SINGLED OUT

NAVIGATING YOUR SEASON OF SINGLENESS

PAULA HALLIDAY

WAVERLEY ABBEY
RESOURCES

Published 2022 by Waverley Abbey Resources, an operating name of CWR, Waverley Abbey House, Waverley Lane, Farnham, Surrey GU9 8EP, UK. Registered Charity No. 294387. Registered limited company No. 1990308.

For a list of National Distributors, visit waverleyabbeyresources.org/distributors

Concept development and editing by Waverley Abbey Resources.
Cover design and typesetting by Esther Kotecha.

Printed and bound in the UK by Page Bros.
Paperback ISBN: 978-1-78951-416-2
eBook ISBN: 978-1-78951-417-9

Honest. Moving. Inspiring. Paula's book does not sugar-coat singleness in the Church. She takes a subject that is caricatured by many and faces it with passion, faith and conviction. The person who enjoys their singleness will be encouraged and relieved to read these words. The person who struggles with their singleness will find words of courage, vulnerability and faith here. Those who are not single will be helped by Paula's powerful challenge not to make assumptions about people who are single. This book is a gift to the Body of Christ.

REV MALCOLM DUNCAN FRSA
AUTHOR; CHURCH LEADER; INTERNATIONAL SPEAKER; THEOLOGIAN

Paula's book calls us to a better understanding of singleness. She writes as a person who has discovered the ways in which churches can so often pigeon-hole single people, but she writes as someone who sees God at the centre of her life and faith. She offers words of encouragement, comfort, strength and hope to all who want to think more deeply about singleness and she calls the church to stand with single people and celebrate them. Her words invite us to let those who are single be honest about where they are and what they feel and she calls us to become churches that are families for all. A word in season for the church today.

DEBBIE DUNCAN
AUTHOR; CHURCH LEADER; NURSE LECTURER; BROADCASTER;
INTERNATIONAL SPEAKER

With unflinching honesty and wry humour, Paula Halliday weaves her own story with profound nuggets of wisdom that will encourage anyone navigating a life that isn't living up to their hopes and expectations. Full of faith-filled wisdom, *Singled Out* will spur you on to fix your eyes on Jesus – not in desperation to get you through while you wait, but in real joy as you see His tender hand at work in the season you are in right now.

NATALIE WILLIAMS, CHIEF EXECUTIVE, JUBILEE+

Thoughtful, provocative and profoundly helpful, this is a vital book for us all. Warm, kind words beautifully entwined with an unmissable message.

JEFF LUCAS, AUTHOR, SPEAKER, BROADCASTER

What a stunning book! Paula bears her heart so vulnerably in the most beautiful way! This book is brimming over with wisdom and godly encouragement, not just for the singleton but for everyone. Paula addresses some topics that are quite frankly awkward to ask a single friend about, yet relieves the tension of the unknown realities that so many people live with but don't talk about. This openness brings clarity for the person who is not single and hope for the one who is! It's really given me insight. Read it, trust me, you need to!

FAITH JARVIS
THE WORSHIP EFFECT DIRECTOR

Paula writes with compelling honesty about her life as a single Christian. Her life has not taken the path that she thought it would and her heartbreak and disappointment is clearly spelled out in *Singled Out*. To make sense of her experiences she delves into the Bible and provides fresh perspectives and deep insight into both well-loved and lesser quoted passages. Whilst she writes this book for other single women, who had thought that they too would be married with a family, I would encourage anyone who wants to fully understand, welcome, value and include single Christians to read Paula's book - she writes from the heart with valuable lessons for all Christians.

AMELIA GOSAL
EXECUTIVE DIRECTOR, SINGLE FRIENDLY CHURCH

If you ever have the pleasure of meeting Paula in real life, you will find her to be funny, honest, warm and generous. As she is in life, she is in her writing. Perhaps you've struggled to talk about singleness with even your closest friends; if that is the case, this book is the conversation you have needed for the longest time, with one who truly cares and truly understands. May it bring you comfort, hope and the wisdom you are longing for.

CHARLOTTE CURRAN
PASTOR, SPEAKER AND AUTHOR OF *DEARLY BELOVED* AND *HOMESICK*

I love the biblical revelation and practical insight that Paula gives us in *Singled Out*. This book is full of great wisdom, good humour and well told stories. Paula is to be commended for being brave and writing about her journey and vulnerabilities in order to help others. I believe *Singled Out* is an important book for everyone to read, so that we can all gain a greater understanding of the complexities of modern life for a single follower of Jesus.

PASTOR ROSS MCBRIDE
LEAD PASTOR, PORTADOWN ELIM

As well as being a wonderfully witty and poignant look at 'singleness', this book offers fantastic insight for anyone finding themselves in 'the middle area of uncertainty', waiting for God's creative answers.

EDWIN MICHAEL
SUPERINTENDENT OF THE ELIM CHURCH IN IRELAND

This book is written by a true follower of Jesus. It is beautifully written from the heart, with a vulnerability which will cause you to both laugh and cry. The principles here will not only be invaluable to those journeying through singleness but also for those who seek to walk with them. This is a much needed book at just the right time. I wholly recommend not just for those who are single, but to anyone who is serious about following Jesus as Paula so obviously does.

JOHN LOWRY
PASTOR, BEERSBRIDGE ELIM CHURCH, BELFAST

DEDICATION

I dedicate this book to you, my friend.
Let's journey this one together.

ACKNOWLEDGEMENTS

My mum and dad... the first people to ever read the words contained within these pages. Thank you for always believing in me, and raising me in a home that loved Jesus. I love you both so much.

Becky, Charmaine, Vic and Janet... I am so thankful for each one of you. Your encouragement, advice and feedback throughout this book-writing process was truly invaluable. And to the rest of my girls... my cheerleaders, my confidants, my prayer warriors and biggest encouragers. Never did I think I could ever write a book, but thankfully He surrounded me with friends who did.

Corey... the man, the myth, the legend. Yay for friends who know how to use a camera. Thank you for capturing a candid moment for this can't-don't girl.

My Pastor, John Lowry... What a support you have been to me over the years. You called something out in me I never knew was there. Jeff Lucas... You may not know me personally, but God used you to play a huge part in my story. Thank you for believing this book was something worth reading.

Rebecca Browne... I so value your input. And the team at Waverley Abbey Trust... It has been an absolute dream to work with you all. Without you, the words in my heart would never have made it into anyone's hand. Thank you.

DC... the left turn I never expected but always wanted. I thank God for you. Thank you for your love and support, your encouragement and wisdom. The adventure continues...

And finally... Jesus. My constant through every season. This one is for you.

CONTENTS

INTRODUCTION

Hey you.

I am so glad you are here.

First of all, if one of your not-so-single friends bought you this very single book, just say, 'Thank you.' It's not nice to throw books at people. That being said, if you wanted to throw this very single book at your not-so-single friend, I don't blame you. I've been there too. Actually, I am there too. Being single is a sensitive topic. And if you want to talk to me about the single life, you better be sure your left hand is missing a sparkly, diamond ring and you are riding the single train right alongside me.

So, before we get started, let's set some things straight.

Yes, I am single.

I am single and in my thirties.

I am single and I don't want to be.

I don't write this book as a girl who *was* single, past tense. No, I am single today. And looking ahead to tomorrow, the relationship forecast isn't looking too hot there either. Single is my current status. And singleness is my current struggle.

Now, I'm no expert. Please no. An expert in singleness is not a title with which I want to be crowned. Not today. Not ever. But single is where I am. And although I may not know you, we share the same status today. So, I feel like I kind of get you and you kind of get me. I'm just another Jesus girl with a whole lot of questions, a pen in my hand and a little bit of faith that God has a plan. For you and for me. So, I write this book as a message to you, but also as a message to me – the one who I think might need to read it most of all.

So, now that we have that cleared up, I invite you to journey with me through these pages. I don't profess to have all the answers, but I do promise to be honest. No sugar-coated struggles. No filtered final cuts. Friend, pull up a chair and let's have a real chat. Years of learning and days of writing and hours of prayer have been poured into these pages for you. Yes, you. This is a safe space. Let's explore this thing together.

I can't wait to see where this goes.

Much love,
Paula
xo

CHAPTER 1

Young [x] Free [x] and Single [✓]

I have been planning this day for a while now. OK, more than just a while. I have been planning this day ever since I was a little girl. And I think about it often. OK, OK, you got me. More than often. I think about it a lot. Yes, I have been beautifully crafting the finer details of this day for many years now.

Delicate lace, the whitest of whites. Simple, yet classy. And the most intricate beading. You know, the kind that glistens every time the sun manages to catch a glimpse of it. Rustic wild flowers will adorn the altar and warm fairy lights will fall from exposed beams in the barn. Shabby, with a splash of chic. Hand-painted wooden pallets will brighten the landscape and homemade decorations will personalise each table. I swear, Pinterest will be so impressed with how those centrepieces turn out. Cutlery will be tied up with hessian and candles will flicker from inside simple glass jars. And there will be baby's breath everywhere. And I mean, everywhere.

Family and friends will choose seats, not sides. And laughter and love will invade the atmosphere as wedding guests fill the church pews. Vows will be exchanged. Promises will be made. Moments will be captured. And precious memories will be stored away, treasured for many years to come. The kind of memories you share with the kids. And the grandkids. And the great-grandkids. There will be singing and dancing and don't forget the food. There will always be food. Lots of food.

More recently, I have imagined the conversations that will be shared. Many will congratulate me. They always knew this day would happen. I will smile and nod along in agreement. Yes, I always thought this day would come. Others will remind me, 'Good things come to those who wait.' I will laugh and make some joke about it; 'Good? It better be great after all this time'. But yes, the wait was definitely worth it. It always is in the end.

But those closest to me, the ones who journeyed this road by my side. Through the highs and the lows. The ups and the downs. The heartbreaks and the heartaches. The waiting and the wanting. The disappointments and sometimes downright despair; they will remind me God always had a plan. A good plan. A perfect plan. And with every fibre of my being, I will add a victorious 'Amen!'. And cheers to that.

This will be a day of celebration. A day to be remembered. One of incredible significance. For this day marks the beginning of all other days to follow. Simply, the introductory paragraph to the next big chapter in my life story. The opening scene to my very own happy ending. The starting block to one of my greatest adventures yet.

This is my dream. I suspect you have yours too. It runs like clockwork and it follows your lead. It keeps to your schedule and adheres to your timing. Every single moment plays out like a beautifully orchestrated piece of music, full of warm tones and sweet-sounding harmonies. The tempo is consistent and the rhythm is steady. And everything weaves together in perfect collaboration. Just as you always planned it would.

As a little girl, it was never a question of *if* this day would come, rather the anticipation of *when*. Falling in love and getting married is not some unrealistic fairy tale or impossible storyline reserved for the movie screens. No, this is just one of those 'ordinary' things, that 'ordinary' people do, as part of their 'ordinary' lives. I believe this to be true because I've watched it unfold in the lives of so many others around me. My parents, my grandparents, my great-grandparents; all following this very same pattern of life. History somehow standardising a sequence for all other life stories to follow. Even today, I watch this repetitive rerun. Friends, close ones and Facebook ones too, extended family members, colleagues, neighbours, the girl behind the counter with the incredible ring. All following a similar pattern. All keeping a similar schedule.

Finish education. Get a job. Fall in love. Get married. Live happily ever after. And maybe have a kid or two. This seems to be the typical order of things. The standard way of life. A pre-written 'to-do' list passed down the generations. And all you have to do is grab a pen and tick off each one in turn. As simple as that.

Yet here I am today; a thirty-something-year-old single Jesus girl clinging on to that same childhood dream and hopelessly hovering my pen over many unchecked boxes. Dashed dreams and jolted plans are difficult for a girl like me to wrap her head – and her heart – around sometimes.

When it comes to church life, I find myself stranded in a weird, middle category. Too old to be classed as a young person. Too young to enjoy any church organisation with a slogan like 'Knitting and Nattering'. Yes, I still want the worship to be loud. Hit that drum as hard as you want. Strum that guitar with all you've got. But I also want to be home and in bed for ten, so don't get too carried away. For sure, I am an adult. I have many, many bills and a slowing metabolism to prove it. But there is always an 'adultier adult' around if you really need some help. You get me?

Modern dating is hard enough to navigate, but Jesus girl plus age doesn't make the simplest equation. For a start, the number of single females in my church far outweighs the number of single males. Yes, I count. With one hand I count. I'm guessing you count too. Actually, it would seem the number of single females across the Church globally far outweighs the number of single males. Either that, or all eligible Christian men attend an underground church somewhere. FYI, if you locate this church, girl you got to let me know. Something tells me we should probably go there together.

But then add age into the equation. Is it just me or do most Christian couples get married in their early twenties? First, we have the childhood sweethearts. The ones who sat beside each other in Sunday school and held hands when it was time to pray.

Everyone always knew they would end up together. Then we have best friends turned soulmates at youth camp. Their parents are also best friends and have been saving for their wedding ever since they were little. And then we have the strangers turned lovers in a whirlwind romance. They met and fell in love at Bible College. Their paths crossed on a mission trip overseas. They were divinely matched on some online dating site. It was an instant connection. Love at first glance. So, they got engaged and married within a year and now have three children under three.

Boy, it's difficult being on the wrong side of the gender imbalance and in the 'overs' category when it comes to age. So very difficult. Now, I don't know what age you are today. You may be in your late teens or early twenties. Maybe you are in your thirties, forties or beyond. But whatever age you are, my guess is you didn't expect to be single today. I get it. Me neither. I didn't expect to be single today either.

Can I be honest with you? I struggle with being single some days. Can I be *really* honest with you? I struggle with being single most days. Absolutely, there are days I allow myself to see beauty in the single life. I mean, no one to consult before booking an impromptu holiday. No one to object to a last-minute road trip with the girls. No need to share snacks with anyone at the cinema. Come on, what's not to love about that? Your food is your food. Your money is your money. Your time is your time and your decisions are your decisions. And some days I am so good at being single. Clear the dance floor. I'm coming through. Beyoncé is my girl and *Single Ladies* is my jam. I will sing loud and I will sing proud and I will wave my ringless left hand in the air without a single care in the world.

But then there are other days when I'm not so good at being single. I struggle with worrying if this season of singleness is actually a life sentence. What if the single life is God's idea of the best life for me? I struggle with feeling like I have messed up somewhere or missed out somehow. The love train has left the station and I am now a permanent resident of Singleville; population of one. I struggle with knowing that time keeps going with no signs of slowing. What an awful rhyme, but one that rhymes true in the deepest parts of my heart. Indeed, the clock keeps ticking and yet I feel no closer to ticking off any of my major life goals. So many 'to-dos'. So very few 'ta-das'. I struggle with waking up in the morning, hopeful today might be the day, only to climb back into bed again at night to nurse the harrowing hurt of disappointment. Today was not the day. Tomorrow doesn't look too good either. I struggle with watching others achieve the dream with ease while I remain on the sidelines, wondering what they did so right and what I did so wrong. I struggle with thinking I am unlovable, unworthy and unpretty, if unpretty were even a word. And feeling all kinds of lonely. Somehow left on the top shelf out of man's reach. Literally. I struggle with waiting. I struggle with wanting. I struggle with wondering; *God, what are you doing here?*

Talk about a whole lot of struggling. But it's real and I know you get it. In moments of strength I reach for my Bible and recall the promises contained within its pages. Promises of purpose. Promises of hope. Promises of a future. Good promises from a good God with good, good plans. Yet, fear grips me. Worry consumes me. Insecurity cripples me. Comparison controls me. Unhelpful perspectives confine me and unhealthy thought patterns restrict me. I'm disappointed and disheartened. I'm weary and worried. I'm so very confused and a whole lot afraid. I guess, I am not that young and I am not that free either. Just single.

So yes, there are days when I'm not so good at being single. Many days. And I've had too many tear-filled conversations with other single Jesus girls to know I am not alone in this struggle. No one really talks about it; the struggle that can come with being single. So it remains the big, fat, silent elephant in the room at family gatherings, the awkward reality of an oddly numbered friendship group and the unspoken prayer of the single heart in a busy church. To those married or in a romantic relationship, the single days are your best days. This is a season to be enjoyed, not endured. Time you will never get back again, so value it. Treasure it. Embrace it. Make the most of it. To many, it is a season crammed with fond memories and happy times. And to some, single is a status to be envied. One they would choose again if given that very chance.

And then, tell the woman who carries the heavy weight of a disappointing health status that you feel the weight of a disappointing relationship status. Explain to the family grieving the loss of a loved one that you are grieving the loss of a love life. Admit to the couple struggling in debt that you are struggling to date. Or the married couple finding their relationship hard, that finding a relationship is the hard part for you. In comparison, our struggles seem small. Our fears seem insignificant. Our hurts seem ridiculous and our tears seem melodramatic. Yet for the single person, the one who never planned for it to be this way; the disappointment is real and the path is difficult to navigate.

The fact we remain single these days is simply unavoidable. Dotted throughout each day are little reminders of the status we have, but do not wish to hold. Another engagement announcement to celebrate. Another wedding invitation to accept. Another form to check Miss, not Mrs. Another night with the girls with no news to share or dateless day to ride solo or third-wheel. Even the ice-cream server knows the deal; 'Was that a single scoop you ordered?' Ugh. Yes, the disappointment is very real and the path is very difficult to navigate.

People encourage us to wait more and want less. I nod because it's polite, not because it's easy. I get the *what*, but please tell me *how*. I need to know *how*. People instruct us to trust more and worry less. Words can be so simple to say, yet so difficult to live, can't they? And others will remind us that some of the Bible greats were single, including Jesus. Bless their hearts. They mean well, but I do despair. These people are seriously looking for a book to the face. A very heavy book.

Friend, I'm not sure how you got to this place today. Maybe you have never been in a relationship before. Instead of dating, you decided to focus on other things like your education or career or serving or travelling. Or maybe the opportunity to date hasn't quite turned up for you yet. Or possibly you are a frequent dater. First dates are common, but second dates are few. Swipe right, yes. Mr Right, no. There may be plenty of fish in the sea but your fish seems to have gone slightly off course. He must be friends with my fish. Or maybe you are the walking wounded of a relationship gone unexpectedly wrong. Once headed in the direction of marriage, life took a sudden twist. A devastating detour. Maybe your left hand came close to wearing that oh-so-sparkly ring. Maybe even wore it once. But now, all you wear is the disappointment of a dream in ruin and the aftermath of a heart-shattering breakup. I have my story. You have yours too.

And although our stories may be different, I think many of us are bound by the same fear – what if our plans remain just that; plans? Written on paper, yet never written into our life stories. I think many of us could settle ourselves today if we knew *one day* everything would fall into place, just as we always planned it would. Imagine that; one day when pen could be put to paper and a very big tick could fill that very empty box. Marriage – check. And on to the next thing. But I simply don't know. I don't know the finer details of my future. I'm not sure many of us do. I hope my story includes a husband, a few children and a white picket fence. But I fear my story involves a lot less husband and a few more cats. This gift of singleness people talk about is the kind of gift I would rather return to sender. I'd much prefer to exchange my present for an express delivery on my future. Please and thank you.

But that's not how life works. So we find ourselves trying to navigate this middle ground. Somewhere between the anticipation of one day and the reality of today. Somewhere between our faith and our fears. Our hopes and our hurts. Our dreams and our disappointments. Somewhere between His perfect plans and our Pinterest plans.

Sometimes I think it's easier to trust God with an unknown future than it is to trust God with a known now. Sometimes it's easier to believe God *will* eventually work all things for good rather than believe He *is* working all things for good. Right here, right now. Today. In this middle ground. Especially when this middle ground doesn't look so good. It's hard to see beyond damaged plans and broken dreams and fractured hopes sometimes. With all the faith I can muster I declare the plans and promises of *one day*, yet struggle to see His plans and promises *today*. I can be so single-minded in my thinking and single-channelled in my focus sometimes.

This middle ground is difficult ground. And I've got to admit, I'm not doing so well walking it right now. But friend, this middle ground is common ground. Let's figure this out together.

There is a beautiful foil print that hangs on my bedroom wall. Its words are written in gold and each letter swirls across the page in pretty, girlie font. It sits perfectly above my bed in a pearly white frame and it simply reads this:

'He has made everything beautiful in its time.'
ECCLESIASTES 3:11

What an incredible verse. It carries such purpose and promise and points a waiting heart to a beautifully creative God with the most impeccable timing. The kind of verse you quote to your friend when she needs encouragement to be patient. A little pick-me-up to trust God when His methods seem strange, His plans seem peculiar and His timing seems off. This verse makes for catchy bumper stickers, pretty bookmarks and cute prints that hang perfectly on bedroom walls. And yet right now, as I tuck into another microwave meal for one and watch another rerun of *The Bachelor*, this verse is much tougher to swallow and harder to digest. Certainly, these words sit well in a frame, but they do not sit so well in the heart of an eagerly expectant Jesus girl who carries the disappointment of a delay, the hurt of a derailed dream and the pain of a life plan gone wrong. Yes, I've always liked this verse. That is, until I have to live in the middle of it. These words do not look as pretty in the dirt and grime of waiting room walls. This promise doesn't look as perfect, or even possible, when all I see are life plans gone wrong and many boxes still left unchecked. And yet, this is God's Word. And God's Word is truth. Something beautiful is the promise of my future. The purpose of His plans. The product of this process. The point of this path. Yours too. But how do we hold tight to this truth today when faced with the imperfections of something incomplete and the ugliness of something unfinished? How do we see beauty in God's plans today when stuck with a status so unwanted, in a season so uncomfortable, for a waiting time so unknown? What are we meant to do when God's idea of a good plan right now is so far away from our imagined ideals and any childhood dream?

Honestly, I don't have all the answers right now. But I do have faith in a God who does. So, with my dream gripped tightly in one hand and this pen held with whatever strength I have left in the other, I choose to believe God has good plans. Perfect plans. Beautiful plans. For you and for me. Does this make being single today easy? Nope, not really. I would change my status in a second if I could. Does this mean I don't struggle? Again, no. I still struggle. And I've got a whole pile of unanswered questions and a bucket-load of single-girl issues in need of a God-sized intervention to prove it. I guess that's why this book is more than just this opening chapter. But when we tuck this truth in our hearts, imprint it in our minds and let it seep deep into our souls, we begin to see God at work right where we are. In this middle ground. Every single day. And dare we believe, every day we are single too.

CHAPTER 2

The Breakup

It was a typical Sunday morning. Thrown together and a little dishevelled, I arrived just in time to hear the opening chords of the first song. I quietly navigated my way through a sea of familiar faces to find our usual seats. And breathe. Church has always been like a second home to me. Just a bunch of imperfect people trying their best to live their individual lives. Each one somehow intertwined and woven together into one big, sometimes dysfunctional, family. Many similarities. Many more differences. Like most families, I guess.

At first, the empty seat beside me came as no surprise. I mean, his timekeeping skills were as good as mine. But as time pressed on and the vacancy remained, I started to wonder where he was. I scanned the congregation once more just to be sure. He sometimes sneaks in and sits closer to the back when running behind schedule. But no, he still wasn't there. My brain rationalised any worry and dissolved any fear. He must have got held up at work again. I was positive everything would be all right. It always is.

The rest of the morning played out much as it always does. Steady pace. Regular rhythm. And I confidently sang along with the music, like a well-known song I had rehearsed hundreds of times before. It was a normal Sunday morning after all. Little did I know of the heartbreak which would interrupt the familiar flow as the day played on.

Doesn't that happen sometimes in life? An unexpected curveball is thrown your way and it flings plans into chaos, hurls hurt in your direction and thrusts life into all kinds of uncertainty and unpredictability. Curveballs do not come with any warning signs. No one sits up ahead and signals for you to dive for cover or brace for impact. No, many moments of life are unforecasted and unscripted and come very much unannounced. This was just another one of those moments. An unexpected curveball tossed towards an unsuspecting me.

I drove to his house blissfully unaware of the conversation to greet me at the door. The look on his face told the story. Something was different. Something wasn't right. Without even saying hello, he sat on the stairs, hands up to his head, and said one sentence that changed my life forever; 'I don't think I can do this anymore.'

Now, I know the words 'changed my life forever' may sound a little dramatic. Possibly a tad extreme. Even as I read these words back to myself, the words I have written, it sounds like an overemotional line from a bad rom-com movie. And all I want to do is throw popcorn at the screen and tell the woman to catch a firm grip of herself. And yet, these are the only words that seem to fit around this moment. The moment the trajectory of my life changed. The moment my life plans unravelled and my dreams were derailed. The moment my hopes were crushed and my goals were shattered and the storyline of my life was permanently altered.

Talk about a curveball. The path I had been carefully treading for almost seven years came to an abrupt stop. I experienced a full one-eighty in a matter of seconds. A change in direction so unexpected, for it pivoted on the words that spilled from his mouth that day.

Dates were not penned in calendars but pencilled in the secret chambers of my heart. Maybe if we got engaged at Christmas, we would be married by the following summer. Plans were not set in stone, but the blueprints were definitely there. And I had an imaginary guest list and private Pinterest board, ready and waiting to go, for when my time finally arrived. I still do. With every passing year, another brick was simply added to the future I was building. The future I always wanted. The future I always expected. The future I always planned. Yes, my groom had been given a name. My future had a familiar face. I certainly never imagined those eight words to be part of my story.

But I don't need to tell you that. You get it. There are unexpected parts to your story too. Curveballs you would rather carve out and details you would rather delete. Moments you never anticipated that came. And moments you always expected that never did. Yet there they are; permanent entries in your life story so far.

The journey back home was strange. Memories we had created together over the years came flooding back, each wave hitting me harder than the last. Anniversaries and holidays. Date days and late nights. A highlight reel of happy times on constant replay in my mind. I thought about the conversations we had shared. The ones where we talked about our hopes and dreams for the future. When we imagined where we might live and argued about the names of our imaginary kids. And when we debated about whether we would get a dog. Or a cat. No, never a cat. Maybe a dog.

After the breakup, family and friends gathered around me for days. Some visited with flowers and even shed tears. It was like we were having some sort of funeral; mourning the death of my 'should-have-been' future and 'could-have-been' dream. Many passed on their condolences. They were sorry to hear the news. And they said kind words; reminding me God's plans are perfect and He promises to work all things together for my good. You know, the usual stuff we say to people following a curveball crisis. For sure, it sounds all so sweet and so very positive, but people simply do not want to hear God is working when life is hurting. I didn't. I didn't want to believe a good God with good plans would allow such a life-altering blow to hit me so badly. Let alone believe He was working in the middle of it. Much less believe He was producing something good from it. It's hard to see how God can bring eventual good when standing in the middle of life's mess, isn't it?

Every part of me struggled to believe their words that day. I was hurting. I was grieving. I was mourning the loss of my 'one day' dream. I wanted to rewrite this part of my story all over again. With complete control of the pen, I would rework the last chapter, add in a plot twist and delete any paragraphs that made me uncomfortable or uneasy. I would omit any unflattering details and reimagine the events which led me to this exact moment. I would edit any errors, wipe out any mistakes, identify any flaws and if needed, flip the entire script. Maybe even illustrate these final pages again. This time only bright, happy colours would fill the blank spaces and only complimentary contrasts would be made. The kind that are just so satisfying to look at and make complete sense. And with a steady hand, not going too close to the edge, all gaps would be filled and finishing touches would be made. No mess ups. No mistakes. Just order and perfection.

I guess if I couldn't alter the ending, I would settle to change the beginning. Start everything all over again on freshly printed blank pages. I mean, if the start is different, the end will be different, right? That way I could recreate the storyline altogether and tell a completely new narrative. Just tweak the content a little and maybe change a character or two. And there you have it; a more beautiful beginning leading to a more beautiful outcome.

But we all know life doesn't work that way. For the first time in my life I finally understood the meaning of the term 'breakup'. This term did not simply refer to the end of our relationship. No, I had to break up with so many things that day. The future I had been building. The plans I had been making. The life I had been dreaming. The goals I had been setting. The list I had been writing. The time frame I had been keeping. All broken. Shattered into a million pieces and scattered like ash right in front of me.

This is the kind of breakup I am talking about.

Not a relationship breakup, although that may be part of it. But the breakup you go through when life plans go one way and life steps go another. The breakup. Or when life 'to-dos' remain unchecked and your dreams and reality have no choice but to separate. The breakup. Or when the heaviness of life's circumstances causes your heart to divide, leaving it shattered in pieces and scattered in unplanned places. The breakup. The kind of breakup that can so easily break you.

People say time is a great healer and I kind of see their point. Time can ease pain. But time alone does not heal pain. Rather, time reveals pain. Time simply exposes where we are hurting most and pinpoints where we need healing most. You see, in time any pain of the relationship breakup subsided, yet I was still hurting. Time did not heal my pain. It simply revealed the true source of it. Disappointment. I was disappointed. Severely disappointed. Disappointed with myself. Disappointed with others. Disappointed with my life. It was so far away from my perfect plans and imagined ideals and fairy tale future. And I was disappointed with God.

How could God allow this to happen? How could God sit back and watch His daughter experience the reality of so many things so very broken?

The hustle and bustle of people coming and going quickly ceased. The visitors stopped. The text messages stopped. The tears dried up and so had the flowers. In my disapproval of recent events, I banished my Bible to the bottom drawer. *Huh; I'll show you, God.*

Like a defiant teenager who didn't get her own way and refused to listen to what He had to say. Seriously, I can be so stubborn at times.

But it hurts when things get broken.

My younger self knows this very well. Allow me to share my 'go-to' story with you. You know, the story you 'go to' in those awkward moments when you have to tell a room full of strangers a fun fact about yourself. This is *that* story.

It was June 1999. A typical Friday night. And I was ten years old.

Now, let's be real for a moment. Ten-year-old Paula was not the girliest of girls. She opted for dirt-filled nails rather than glittery polish, wore tracksuits instead of dresses and chose boyish trainers over delicate slip-ons. Comfort over fashion. Every. Single. Time. The fact I write these words with unpolished, chipped nails, dressed in an oversized hoodie and baggy sweat bottoms, with hair scraped back in a messy bun, tells me I haven't changed all that much. And I don't mean one of those Instagram-worthy messy buns. I mean, unbrushed chaos wrapped in a hair bobble and perched on the top of a very unwashed head. What a visual. And definitely not a description I would recommend using on any online dating profile, in case you are wondering.

But anyway. Growing up, my family lived at the top of a very steep hill. I repeat. A *very* steep hill. For a not-so-girlie girl like me, this was the dream. A fun-filled, adrenaline-pumping slope right at my front door. Amazing. Just grab your bike and off you go. Adventure truly awaits. There was just enough time to check the coast was clear before freewheeling to the bottom at lightning fast speed. Okay, maybe not lightning fast speed. But it sure felt like it. I had timed this stunt perfectly. It had been executed with flawless precision many times before. A quick glance over the metal safety railing to make sure no traffic had filtered off the main road, and just go for it. You didn't even have to pedal. Just let gravity do its thing. Exhilarating. Did I mention this hill was steep? Yes, very steep.

But this was not a day for bikes. Oh no. This was a day for rollerblades. Do you see where this is going? I assumed the only starting position I knew how. Bent knees. Arms held firmly in brace position. I completed my final check over the railing, and released. The roller-skates gained momentum like never before. But against all odds, I stopped just before reaching the bottom of the very steep hill. And breathe. Weren't expecting that were you? I gained my composure for just a moment. One final glide to cross the imaginary finish line and victory would be mine.

But times of adventure can be so easily interrupted by unexpected moments, can't they? So can typical Sunday mornings. And on this occasion, this unexpected moment came in the form of a very unseen footpath. In seconds, my confident last stride turned into a catastrophic nose dive. I landed in the middle of the road in a pitiful heap.

I squealed, and I mean squealed. So loud in fact, unsuspecting neighbours emerged from their homes with towels. I don't know what they expected to see. I can only assume the noise of my cries echoed into their once peaceful homes and called them into immediate action. You know what they say; if there is an emergency, make sure to grab a towel. OK, nobody says that. But hey, I needed a towel. I needed many, many towels.

The result of the accident was obvious. No need for a medical background to know what was wrong. Not one, but two arms, were badly broken. And the momentum of the fall had carried me across the gravel road, leaving one side of my face badly cut, swollen and bruised. Ouch.

Yes, it hurts when things get broken. Really hurts. And I know that same pain today. I'm guessing you do too. Instead of badly broken arms, a bruised face and the painful injuries of an unexpected fall, many of us know what it's like to have badly broken dreams and a bruised heart and experience painful injuries from an unexpected curveball. Yes, many of us know the pain of a breakup. Maybe you have never thought of it this way before. But I think this is why being single can be so hard at times. We are experiencing a breakup. Many, many breakups.

My Bible remained tucked away in the bottom drawer for a number of days. Instead of praying, my thoughts simply wondered did God even care about the breakups I was facing. I think many of us girls wonder that. Does God see *this* kind of hurt? Does God actually care about something like this? For many of us, it's easy to grasp how God, the Creator of the universe, would be concerned with 'big' world issues. Poverty. War. Disease. Injustice. Of course, each one moves the heart of God. But this? A relationship breakup of sorts? A strained hope for a husband? A torn up 'to-do' list with so many unchecked boxes? A crushed expectation and a shattered dream, so far off from delicate lace, a picket white fence and that eagerly anticipated beautiful ending? Seems a little small. A lot less significant, if you ask me.

And yet, it was this kind of breakup that was breaking me. Every tear-soaked pillow yearned to know: *God, do you care? God, do you care about this?* I thought my life would look different by now. *God, do you care?* Still the empty seat beside me in Church. *God, do you care?* Just the odd-one-out at family gatherings. Still the odd number in a friendship circle. *God, do you care?* Always the bridesmaid, never the bride. Always the wedding guest, without a plus-one. *God, do you care?* Another first date, and yet never a second. Another year older with the same last name. *God, do you care? God, do you care about this?*

I drew a large X through my pre-set life plans and I drew away from God. Disappointment does that. It creates distance if left unchecked. But things just don't look as clear from faraway, do they? Disappointment blurs our focus. It shifts our gaze and it alters how we see God. Disappointment distorts truth. It allows what we see to dictate what we believe about God, rather than allow what we know about God to dictate what we see.

Finally, I reached for my Bible. Not because I wanted to. Oh no. I was still confused and very much annoyed with God. I never told Him that, but hey; He's God. I guess the silent treatment didn't fool Him anyway. But the deep longings of my disappointed soul knew His words were exactly what I needed to hear. I needed truth. Not momentary facts. Not changeable feelings. Not other people's opinions or even my own thoughts. I needed truth. Life-giving, hope-filled words of truth that can only be found within the pages of two worn-out Bible covers.

I flicked through its pages and found a safe place to land in Jeremiah 18. It says this:

'So I went down to the potter's house, and I saw him working at the wheel. But the pot he was shaping from the clay was marred in his hands; so the potter formed it into another pot, shaping it as seemed best to him. Then the word of the LORD came to me. He said, "Can I not do with you, Israel, as this potter does?" declares the LORD. "Like clay in the hand of the potter, so are you in my hand, Israel."'

JEREMIAH 18:3-6

Boy, did I feel like this clay. I still do sometimes. Broken clay. Just a disappointed woman whose make-up is a whole heap of breakups.

I imagine sitting with you right now. We might laugh about the single life. Maybe share a story or two. And you would subtly hint I should probably watch some online tutorial on how to improve the messy bun look. You know, in a you-don't-look-terrible-but-you-could-look-better kind of way. Girl, you are so sweet. I might tell you of a special moment I shared with some guy at the supermarket once upon a time. Our eyes locked for a whole five seconds. And I'm pretty sure his hand touched mine as we both reached for the frozen peas. It was a Hallmark movie kind of moment. That is, if Hallmark movie kind of moments ever happened to girls like me. They don't. But then in a moment of honesty and unguarded vulnerability, we would admit to one another we struggle to see God clearly sometimes. It's hard to see God in the middle of many breakups. And although we might never admit it, there is a part of us that simply wants to know. Actually, there is part of us that needs to know, if God even cares? Does He care about something like this?

So back to my 'go-to' story. To a room full of strangers, my story usually ends with the accident. I am the girl who broke both arms rollerblading. I am the girl who masterfully navigated her way down a very steep hill, only to trip on the tiniest of footpaths and obtain rather dramatic injuries. But to you my friend, there is more to the story. There always is. Honestly, the finer details of this day are somewhat a blur. And I may have used creative licence over the years to make it more exciting. Instead of tripping on a footpath, maybe I skilfully swerved to avoid a head-on collision with a double-decker bus. Or instead of a steep hill, maybe I descended a death-defying, mountain-sized slope with cliff-like edges and razor-sharp turns. Sounds way more impressive that way. But the truth is, I don't remember much about the accident. I don't remember the neighbours' faces or the colour of their emergency towels. I don't even remember much of the pain. But what I do remember is this: when my dad arrived at the hospital.

There I was, helplessly sprawled across an uncomfortable hospital bed in a darkened corridor, when he finally arrived. I have no idea where he was that night. Maybe he was at work. Or possibly a football game. In that moment, it didn't matter. All that mattered was he was there. And this is when the unthinkable happened. No amount of pain or discomfort could distract my young eyes from what they would see next. His eyes began to well up. His voice started to shake. And all of a sudden, tiny droplets trickled down his flushed cheeks. This was the first time I'd ever seen my dad cry. Ever.

This was new. Unexpected. Little ten-year-old Paula didn't think this was possible. Weren't dads supposed to be strong and sturdy and stable individuals who remained completely unfazed by life and immune to these kinds of emotions? Oh, how wrong was I. You see, when my dad looked at me, his little girl; he saw the brokenness and the bruises, the hurt and the hopelessness, the pain and very many shattered pieces. He saw it all. I guess, he felt it too. And this moved him to tears. Every droplet that fell down his cheeks that day simply pointed a hurting daughter to her father's heart. A father's heart that deeply cared.

Do you know Jesus was moved to tears over a breakup once? Tucked away in John 11:35 is the shortest verse recorded in Scripture. Just two simple words. *'Jesus wept'*. Imagine that; Jesus, God incarnate, shed tears. Over what? Poverty? War? Disease? Injustice? You might think, but no. Not this time. These tears were reserved for a woman who experienced the disappointment of a breakup. Here's what happened. In John 11 we read of two sisters, Martha and Mary. Two different sisters with one important thing in common. They both loved Jesus. He was one of their closest friends. So when Lazarus, their brother, was sick, the sisters did what they only knew how and sent word to their friend Jesus.

Makes sense, doesn't it? These two women had witnessed countless miracles at His hand before. The hungry were fed, the blind could see and the sick were remarkably restored. He was on everyone's speed-dial for a miracle. They knew Jesus could do something to fix this. Surely He would do something to fix this. Yes, they had a plan. A checklist of sorts. *Call for Jesus – check.* Yes, they had a time frame. *Jesus, come quickly – check.* Yes, they had an abundance of faith and a bucket load of hope. *Check and check.* And yet, the smell of decay escaped from shut tomb walls before Jesus ever arrived. Oh, did these two sisters know the pain of a breakup. Things didn't turn out like they planned. Their timings were way off too. Their hopes were shattered and their expectations were in pieces.

Two sisters.

Two hurting hearts.

But two very different responses.

You see, when Jesus finally arrived, four days after Lazarus' death, Martha ran to meet Him. Hope still simmered deep in her heart. She knew Jesus could turn this situation around for good. But Mary; she stayed at home. Her hope had dried up and nearly died out. Instead of running to Jesus, she withdrew from Jesus. Both sisters were grieving. Both sisters were hurting. Both sisters were experiencing a breakup. And yet, one sister runs to Jesus, the other retreats from Jesus.

Is it possible this is why Jesus wept? I think so. You see, Jesus always knew Lazarus' story would far outlive the grave he lay in that day. To Him, their brother was just 'sleeping' (John 11:11). Jesus was not mourning the death of soon-to-be-living Lazarus. No, I think Jesus' tears were for Mary. A woman who felt the disappointment of a breakup. Each tear that fell down Mary's cheek represented an unfulfilled hope. An unmet expectation. An unanswered prayer. An unchecked plan. Jesus saw each one. When her calls of faith turned to cries of despair, Jesus heard them too. When disappointment drove distance between Him and Mary and the pain of a breakup caused her to break away. Jesus felt it. He was moved by it; and so He wept. What a beautiful thought.

I wonder if you, too, sit surrounded by many broken things today. Maybe you sit in ash of former plans and in despair of future plans. Me too. Yes, me too. As if looking in a mirror, I see your broken pieces, your breakups, as a reflection of my own. I see it in you, because I see it in me. It's not always obvious and we can hide it so very well. But often hidden behind any light-hearted joke or rehearsed, 'I'm fine' is a heavy heart full of disappointment that things are the way they are and not the way you planned them to be. Hidden behind casual smiles are captive tears and hope-filled dreams are hurt-filled hearts. I know the pain is there, because I feel it too. Maybe not every day, but enough days to feel the niggle of discomfort, the nag of discontent and the desperate need to somehow understand God cares and has a better plan.

Sweet friend, I get it. It hurts when things get broken. But we have a Father today who cares deeply about what breaks us. It's true; we do live in a broken world. And in a broken world, things get broken. Mankind's gift of free choice in the Garden of Eden welcomed sin into the world, and with sin came brokenness. A package deal which was never God's intention. Simply the consequence of sin that can, and will, be part of our life stories this side of eternity. But just like when my dad arrived at the hospital that day, our Heavenly Father sees our broken plans and bruised hearts, our painful breakups and very many shattered pieces. He sees them all. He feels them too. And this moves His heart. Maybe even to tears.

It is possible your view of God is somehow tainted by your relationship with your earthly father. Maybe this relationship is damaged, distant or non-existent. Maybe your dad wasn't there for you when you fell and broke a bone or scraped your knee. Or maybe he abruptly told you that those little things of life, those things that caused you to cry or worry, weren't actually a big deal. Maybe the mere thought God would be interested in something like your relationship status sounds ridiculous to you. But when it comes to your Heavenly Father, if it concerns you, it concerns Him. If it breaks your heart, it breaks His heart too.

In a broken world, we cannot control the breakups we face. But we can control our response to them. We do still have a choice. Run to Him or retreat from Him. I have seen the disappointment of singleness drive many Jesus girls to distance themselves from Him. There is no judgment here. Hey, remember the banished Bible in the bottom drawer? I've been there too, but I refuse to stay there.

So, what if we allowed our disappointments to draw us closer to God, not further away? Would we see our breakups differently? I think so. You see, closeness to God brings clarity to circumstances. Nearness brings new perspective. Intimacy brings fresh insight. When we draw close to God, no longer do we draw our own conclusions. Instead, we see things from His perspective. A Father's perspective. A Potter's perspective. Broken things are the beginning of beautiful things when placed into the right hands. He sees potential in the broken pieces and endless possibilities to remake our breakups into something good. Something beautiful.

When you know the heart of the Father, you trust the hand of the Potter. Friend, He is the Potter. Powerful enough to recreate something beautiful from our breakups. But what may be even sweeter still to a girl's hurting heart; He is also our Father. Personal enough to care. And maybe shed a tear or two.

Anyway, I better sort this messy bun look out. I'm off to the supermarket to hover around the frozen peas. Maybe today is the day for my Hallmark movie moment.

CHAPTER 3

Unexpected Detours to Unimaginable Destinations

The tram was packed with all kinds of people. Families gathered together in little huddles as they planned their daily itineraries. Teenagers crowded around exit doors as they listened to their music way too loudly. Businessmen crouched over small centre tables as they vigorously typed on their daily commute. While other passengers slept. And then, two young(ish) women from Belfast on a last-minute city break.

With hands wrapped around a pocket-sized map and hearts brimming with uncontainable excitement, we jumped on the tram with one destination in mind. Prague Castle. Everyone on board was headed the same direction too. So when the driver firmly placed his foot on the brakes, left his seat and announced something rather loudly in Czech, confusion washed over our faces. Puzzled and perplexed. I didn't know a single word in Czech. Neither did she. We only spoke English and a little bit of high-school French. But what use was, 'Hello, my name is Paula and I like to go swimming at the weekends' to me now? Whatever the driver proclaimed, it sounded important. Really important.

Our suspicions were confirmed when people frantically gathered their belongings to make a swift exit. We hesitated. Should we get off or should we stay on? We didn't know. So we engaged in a little routine: stand up – look outside – sit back down – repeat. You know, in a you-look-like-you-are-doing-something-but-you-are-actually-avoiding-doing-anything kind of way. I guess we hoped at some point one of us might suddenly, and quite miraculously, understand Czech and know exactly what the driver had said. Kind of like the tower of Babel, only in reverse.

We watched others to see if this might help. Most people got off. But some people stayed on. Only to make our decision a whole lot harder. What if the driver had said, 'If you want to go directly to Prague Castle, please stay on board' and we got off. How inconvenient and frustrating would that be? But what if we remained seated and the unfamiliar rhythm of the driver's words proclaimed, 'If you want to avoid going to Prague Castle and experience a never-ending tram journey to the depths of utmost despair, then buckle up.' Now that is bad. And not at all what we signed up for. But before we could decide for ourselves, the doors abruptly shut and the wheels began to turn. Great. A never-ending tram journey to the depths of utmost despair it is then.

Initially, things looked promising and it appeared as though we were headed straight for the castle. Our dream destination. But in one swift motion the tracks jolted and we dramatically veered left, only for the dream to slowly shrink to the size of a holiday postcard.

I guess some journeys just take unexpected detours.

Unexpected detours, to unknown destinations, for an unknown length of time.

Soon after the breakup, any money I had saved for future days was spent on buying my first house. Instead of delicate white lace, exposed barn beams and beautiful floral arrangements, I splashed my cash on a hefty deposit, brand-new furniture and a fresh lick of paint. To many, this was an extravagant purchase. An expensive comeback after a curveball crisis. But to me, this two-storey, three-bedroom home was an investment. And the garden; well, it created space for my maybe-one-day dog too.

I stepped into this new season filled with anticipation. I thought; maybe not today, but one day, and one day soon, I will live here with my future family. Settle here with my spouse. Lodge here with my little ones. This house was not just a building made of brick and mortar. This was a fresh start. A clean slate. Somewhere to rebuild my broken dreams once again. A different-new beginning for my same-old beautiful ending. Or so I thought.

At this point in our journey together, I want to give you an update on where I am with the whole single thing. Are you ready for this? Brace yourself. There are no updates. And there ends that story. Cue the tumbleweed and a sombre symphony with an orchestra of tiny violins. Yes, I am still single. Just a few first dates wiser, a couple of online dating attempts later and four years older than when I first unexpectedly landed in the deserted shores of Singleville. Four years older. *Four.* Yup. A lot of time has passed between two chapters, right?

Indeed, I feel the jolt of an unexpected detour. I understand the panic of an unknown destination. And I know the aggravation of an unknown time frame. Ugh. I'm still riding the single train (or tram) right alongside you. Honestly, I thought things would be different by now. I hoped things would be different by now. I prayed things would be different by now. And yet, I remain unmoved. Stuck on one of those uncomfortable tram seats with some strange man shouting things at me I do not understand.

Get off or stay on? We still didn't know which decision was the right decision. We smiled and we laughed and we joked. But smiles and laughs and jokes can often mask the panic of a confused heart. I know that too well. Believe me. I much prefer light-hearted conversations to deep intellectual debates. I will fill all awkward silences with equally awkward, yet witty, comments. Yes, all awkward silences. Every. Single. Last. One. And I will make fun of myself before you might ever get the chance. So, when people ask me for love life updates, humour is my first line of defence. With my sword of sarcasm and my breastplate of banter, I am ready and armed with my rapid response. Maybe my prince charming is having navigational difficulties. Or he is out there, somewhere, on his very white, very injured horse. Oh yes. Smiles and laughs and jokes can truly mask the panic of a confused heart. They can. And they do.

Can I be vulnerable with you for a moment? Take off my mask and simply bare all? Just one single Jesus girl to another. I know God has good plans for my life. The Bible-believing, Jesus-loving, Sunday school-going, good-Christian part of me knows this very well. But the human part of me, she invites fear and doubt into the equation. As time moves on and circumstances do not, fear and doubt can slowly strangle truth of its power and choke it to the brink of death. You wouldn't be alone if you thought that when you ran to God with your breakups, He would fix them quickly and things would somehow turn out exactly as you always expected they would. I did. And yet, four years later, my dreams seem further away today than ever before. The promise of something beautiful seems so far away from the reality of something still very broken. Under this mask hides a woman deeply afraid that God's good plans might take her to places she doesn't want to go. Let alone stay. Hidden beneath any freshly painted smile is a woman thankful He cares to take her breakups. Yet frightened He might choose to remake each one into something she doesn't want. Or maybe even like. And secretly concealed by any glossy exterior is a woman so very scared to admit that she has often wondered if God's good plans might not be as good as the ones she originally devised herself. Ouch. It's not easy being so vulnerable and exposed. Or attractive. But it's real. I just wish honesty didn't look so ugly.

It's hard to imagine better plans than our own sometimes. But aren't God's ways higher than our ways and His thoughts higher than our thoughts (Isaiah 55:8–9)? I underline these words in my Bible, yet I struggle to align these words to my single heart sometimes. But friend, let me highlight this truth for you today; it's hard to imagine better plans than our own, because God's plans are unimaginably better. Our human hearts are restricted. We cannot fully comprehend the height of His ways. Our earthly desires are confined by earthly limits, standards and norms. We struggle to delve into the depths of His desires for us. Even our greatest imaginations are limited by our own thoughts and ideas. But His plans for us are inconceivable. His purposes for us are incomprehensible. And sometimes this means our journeys will take unexpected detours. Yes, unexpected detours to unimaginable destinations.

In Jeremiah 1:5, it says:

> 'Before I formed you in the womb I knew you,
> before you were born I set you apart.'

The term 'set apart' means to 'be separated' or, in other words; 'singled out'. Yes, you are singled out. Me too. Before we were known by others, we were fully known by God. He set plans for our lives long before we ever set foot on Earth. When we were but a seed in our mother's womb, our Heavenly Father had good plans for us. When we were but dust of the Earth, the Potter knew exactly what He wanted to do with us. And so today, He is moving us and directing us and guiding us as seems best to Him (Jer. 18:4). Friend, there are places He wants us to go, goals He wants us to achieve and dreams He wants us to reach. And although the finer details and logistics are often unknown to us, they are fully known to God. So, He lovingly sets the co-ordinates of our lives and points us in the direction of a beautiful ending.

Now I know this sounds good. I mean, sign me up for a beautiful ending. But words on paper don't always translate so easily into words in practice. His beautiful ending certainly sounds good, until you realise it might take you down routes you never expected to go, direct you down paths you never intended to tread and land you in places you never imagined you might live.

I delve into my Bible and I recite verses like Psalm 37:4 in my prayers:

> 'Take delight in the LORD and he will give you
> the desires of your heart.'

You know, a little reminder to God in case He forgot it was in there. Certainly, a promise to declare when persistent prayers for a partner remain unanswered and deep-rooted desires for a relationship remain unfulfilled. An anthem for dateless days and single seasons and curveball comebacks and tram journeys that unexpectedly turn left, right? But how often do we miss a beautiful truth because we simply misinterpret the text? You see, although I have read this verse many times before, I have really only ever read *my* version. The one that goes a little something like: 'When I enjoy the Lord, everything will eventually work out the way I always planned it would'. Ah yes, I can almost hear the irregular trot of my man's injured, white horse in the distance! Or maybe a bit more like this: 'When I delight myself in Him, He will give me exactly what I want, exactly how I want it and exactly when I want it'. (Psalm 37:4, the Paula Halliday Singles Edition). Erm, I'll take one tall, dark and handsome male to go, thank you very much.

But when I studied this verse, I uncovered something important that us girls really need to grasp. The word 'delight' in the original text means 'to bend'. Now that changes things. My version certainly never mentioned anything about bending. And for a girl who can barely touch her toes without feeling the discomfort of a stretch and the pain of a reach, the idea of bending my desires right now sounds rather unpleasant. And uncomfortable. And uneasy. And unattractive. Maybe even downright impossible. Don't you think?

But that's what it means to 'take delight in the Lord'. It means your desires somehow bend according to His desires. Your plans are made pliable to His plans, your heart is softened by His heart, and your cravings are carved by Him alone. Us Jesus girls can run into all kinds of trouble when we misunderstand a promise of God. He is not some sort of genie-god that grants our every wish, adheres to our every request and keeps to our every schedule. And if we believe the precious words of this promise to mean He will bend to our desires, and our order for one tall, dark and handsome male to go, is automatically being processed, we set ourselves up for a whole lot of confusion. Distant dreams and disappointing detours can so easily make us doubt His presence (where He is), His person (who He is), His provision (what He does), His plans (how He does it), His pace (when He does it) and His promise (what He says). Believe me, four years is a long time for a girl to ask questions.

But here is the truth; God does promise to give us the desires of our heart. But first, we must bend to align our desires with His. Now, let me be the first to say, all this talk of bending makes me feel a tad uncomfortable. I guess that's because the same girl who struggles to bend and touch her toes, struggles to bend in a spiritual sense too. I have to admit, my desires are pretty fixed in position. On the one hand, I want God's good plan for my life. I really do. But on the other hand, I want my good plan too. And I want it now. So, what if these two simply don't match up? Do I really want to go where He is taking me today, if it means I embark on a journey filled with unplanned stops and unpleasant turns and unknown details? Or worse, what if I never end up where I want to go? Forever a Miss, and I miss out on marriage completely? Oh, how I feel the pull of my heartstrings between 'yes Lord, I want your good plans' and 'just as long as somewhere on route, and sometime soon, I disembark the single tram and get myself a husband'. Ouch. I feel the stretch. The strain. The stress. The struggle. The pull. The tension. Between wanting the good plans He promises and the good plans I propose.

But if I truly want the deepest desires of my heart fulfilled, something has got to give. Something has got to bend. And that something has got to be me. What about you? Friend, I don't want to imply this is easy. It most certainly is not. Especially when His idea of a good plan right now means we remain travel companions on the single tram. I get it. It's hard. But I do choose to trust God. And that's exactly what King David instructs us to do too. To 'Trust in the LORD' (Psa. 37:3).

Now, before you go throwing this book at someone, I know how simple this seems. And girl, if we had a date for every person who has ever told us to trust God, right? So easy to say. Not so easy to live. But over the past four years, as I have learnt to come to God with my breakups – not once, not twice, but every time the reality of singleness reminds me that my plans are still broken – He draws me close and reminds me His plans are always better.

When we choose to run to God, we might not know all the details.

But we will know Him. And when we know Him – *truly* – know Him, we trust Him. You see, God is both great and good, wise and kind, faithful and perfect, all-knowing and all-powerful, Father and Potter. Knowing *who* God is reminds us of *why* He can be trusted. Allow what you know about God to narrate your journey. Allow your faith in Him to loosen your firm hold on what you always wanted or planned, finger by finger, so you can fully grasp hold of all He wants for you. Allow your faith in Him to release your grip of 'good', so you can grab onto His promise of better. Yes, knowing *who* God is frees us from needing to know every future detail. Because we trust the One who does.

Okay, but how?

Friend, I get it. This advice isn't new. But sometimes, it isn't the advice that needs to change. It is our practice of it that does. To trust God is good advice. The right advice. But I think what we all really want to know is *how*. How are we supposed to trust God when stuck on this single tram going to who knows where, for who knows how long, for who knows why, with so many voices shouting who knows what? How are we supposed to remember God's plans are better when our plans are still broken?

Sometimes we need something physical to help jog our memories, don't we? Safely tucked away above my bedroom wardrobe, I have a memories box. You know, a box to keep my memories in. A memories box. This box overflows with cherished cards and special letters. Precious photographs and priceless autographs. Newspaper cut outs and school report cards. Used concert tickets and stamped boarding passes. And, wait for it: three extracted adult teeth in a small, crumpled, white envelope.

That's right. Three. Extracted. Adult. Teeth. In an envelope. Classy. For fear of sounding completely ridiculous, there used to be four teeth in said box, but one is now proudly displayed on my friend's fireplace. True story; but one for another time I guess.

This box holds my memories, because my mind simply fails to. It stores my significant life treasures. Little life gems. Important life mementos. Each treasure, its own story and each gem, its own significance. Precious enough to keep. Important enough to store away, not throw away. Well, maybe not the teeth. But I'm kind of attached to them now. Anyway, every single item signifies a moment in history, a milestone in my story I want to remember. I need to remember.

Yes, sometimes we need something physical to help us remember something important. I think the same is true in a spiritual sense. Sometimes we need something physical to remind us we can trust God.

Do you know God instructed the Israelites to get a memories box too? Well, memorials. But that's just an ancient version of a memories box. You see, God knew the Israelites needed to be reminded to trust Him too. History reveals they were experts in the field of forgetfulness. In Exodus 14 we read how God miraculously transformed Red Sea waves into a bone-dry walkway. Can you imagine? Incredible. And yet, the Israelites reached the other side only to doubt God's ability to provide basic food and fresh water. A simple flick of the page. The next chapter in their story. The next stop in their journey. And their faith was shaken and their fear was rising. Fear forgets what faith has seen.

Somehow their immediate needs diminished their faith in His provision and power, His goodness and greatness. Somehow their present struggles made them forget their past successes. It's true. Yesterday's victories can easily dim in light of today's challenges. God's faithfulness can fade fast in the shadow of current fears. God's good plans don't seem so good when food is limited and water is bitter. Or when lying in a hospital bed with broken arms and broken dreams. Or when the tram jolts left and your dreams stay right. In uncertain times, fear can fog our memory, doubt can drain our faith and confusion can cloud our judgment.

And that's why God commanded the Israelites to gather memorials. To start a memories box. Here's what happened: as a result of their forgetfulness, the Israelites embarked on a forty-year-long journey. Forty years wandering in the wilderness simply equalled forty years wondering if God could still be trusted. Let's just say, God needed to remind them a whole lot of times. But at the end of this forty-year walk, the Israelites were confronted with another vast and impassable body of water, the River Jordan (Josh. 3). Once again, waves split and the Israelites walked to the other side, completely unharmed. And look what God commanded His people to do when they reached the other side this time:

'Take up twelve stones from the middle of the Jordan, from right where the priests are standing, and carry them over with you and put them down at the place where you stay tonight."

JOSHUA 4:3

Did you catch that? God commanded His people to gather stones from the middle of the River Jordan and carry each one to the other side with them. Why? Because each stone would be a physical reminder to trust God, because He has never failed them before. A reminder of who God was and, therefore, who God is. A constant memorial of what God *was* capable of and, therefore, what God *is* capable of. A visual prompt to point their fear-filled hearts to His sea-splitting power and unfailing faithfulness. A signpost to His timely intervention and innovative tactics. A landmark of His goodness in difficult times and His greatness in times thought impossible. And boy, did the Israelites need this reminder. Because just up ahead lay their next big challenge. Jericho. A strong walled city swarmed with even stronger warriors. A challenge so big it had potential to instil fear and doubt and cause them to run. But can you imagine what the Israelites would have seen if they chose to follow their fear and run away from Jericho? Stones. Stones from the River Jordan. Stones to remind them to trust God. For if God can split seas, He can certainly flatten walls and conquer cities too.

God knew the Israelites needed these stones. He knows we need stones too. Friend, there will be times in life when circumstances scream so loud, it will be hard to hear His voice. There will be seasons when struggles feel so heavy, it will be difficult to feel His presence. There will be unexpected detours, to unknown destinations, for an unknown length of time, that may cause us confusion. Fear. Panic. Doubt. There will be dateless days and lonely nights and many times we will want to take matters into our hands. And that's why it's so important we revisit a time when we heard God clearly; when we felt His presence close and when we saw His mighty hand move. We must learn to recall those times when He proved Himself faithful and know with complete assurance, He is faithful still. As we sit today surrounded by many life uncertainties, stuck with an unwanted status, overwhelmed by unanswered questions, our plans still broken, we must rewind to remind ourselves that God can be trusted. And mark it with a stone.

You might have to dig around a little, but I promise, you will find one. Buried in your past is a milestone in your story. Something to remind you of why God can be trusted right now with your single status. And when you find this stone, tuck it safely in your heart. Store it in a box. Write it in your journal. Share it with a friend. Get it tattooed on your forehead. Okay, maybe not. But do something physical to help you remember. So, when life throws you a curveball or takes an unexpected detour, you can reach for your memories box. Dust it off. Delve into its contents. Look through your collection of precious stones and remind yourself all over again. Yes, God can be trusted.

You see, when you know Him, you trust Him. And when you trust Him, bending your desires to align with His doesn't sound like such a bad idea after all. Now before we move on, I want to show you how this whole stone-gathering exercise has helped me. Here are a couple of stones I have collected throughout my life. And, let's be honest, I have needed to polish these off a time or two over the past four years.

Stone #1

It didn't take long for my childhood dream of becoming a Disney princess to dissolve in the real world of adulthood. So, I set my heart on something else. Something less glamorous and a lot more realistic. Social work. I was going to become a social worker. What a great plan, said I. I studied hard and I achieved good grades. I obtained an interview and I prepared well. I even prayed too. Only for a beautifully crafted letter to spell out one word. Rejection. It's never easy when you fall flat at the last hurdle. And I fell hard.

How one moment so easily disrupted my life goals and interrupted my life plans. The tracks definitely jolted and once again, I veered left. Hard left. No seat belt. No plan B. Yes, rejection is hard. But, dear friend, it is not the end. And it wasn't the end for me. I didn't know it then, but what looked like a rejection was simply a God interjection. An unexpected detour down a different track. A better track. Hindsight is a wonderful thing, isn't it? Only now do I realise, if they did awards for the world's worst social worker I would be crowned winner every single time. Like, seriously. I cope much better in a world where furniture might sing and wildlife might clean, than be immersed in the difficult reality many social workers face today. Yes, social work is a good job. It's just not a good job for me. I know that now. But God knew that then. And so I cut a stone out of this rejection letter. I carve a stone from this closed door. I place a stone at this life detour. And I remind myself today that God knows me way better than I know myself. And sometimes my idea of a good plan isn't actually a good plan for me at all.

When I look at this stone, no longer do I see a sharp left turn as an interruption in my journey, rather as an invitation to go right where God wants me to be. No longer do I see a closed door, rather a redirection to an open door elsewhere. A career in speech and language therapy is a much better fit for a girl who loves words, both spoken and written. No longer do I see a brick wall blocking my life goals and stopping my life plans. Rather, I see a wall made of precious stone. Detours are not dead ends. Detours are not denials. Detours are dreams set by God in a different direction than what we could ever have imagined for ourselves. Friend, single seasons are hard to make sense of when that's all we see right now. That's why we need a stone to look back to. A reminder today to trust God, for His plans are always better. Unimaginably better.

Stone #2

After the breakup, I conducted a life post-mortem. We tend to do that after life curveballs and unexpected detours, don't we? We analyse every decision, revisit every word, evaluate every action and scrutinise every reaction, which led us to that precise moment. The moment the curveball came flying. The moment the tracks jolted. We do this in the hopes we might pinpoint exactly where things went wrong. We then draw a line from our current disappointment to our past, only to feel guilt over 'must-have-been' mistakes, shame over 'must-have-been' wrong turns and regret over 'must-have-been' missed opportunities.

Seven years is a long time to be in a relationship. Seven years is an even longer time to be in a wrong relationship. Many times I have wondered if I made a wrong decision somewhere. Maybe I stayed on too long or maybe I got off too early. Either way, I'm now stuck on the single tram and I just have to go wherever it takes me.

I could look back at the breakup and recall the moment my life plans crumbled. Or, instead, I could look back at the breakup and realise there is a stone to be uncovered. Not all life gems instantly sparkle. Some are found deep in the dirt of our disappointments. In the muck of our mistakes. In the soil of our hardest struggles. Some stones just need a little time to shine. A splash of polish to reveal their true beauty. A painful process to unearth their lasting goodness.

Four years ago I struggled to see God's good plan. Instead of a stone, I simply saw an unwanted moment that rocked my world and tore straight through my hopes and dreams. Sometimes it is only when we look back a little further down the road, that we see God's goodness speckled in the grief. Only now do I realise the breakup was the best thing for both of us. He was on his journey. I was on mine. They just happened to be going in opposite directions. I know that now. But God knew that then.

God's desires for us don't always look desirable to us to begin with. But this stone reminds me to trust God anyway. For He is the One who sees our breakups and promises to remake each one into something better. He can rework any mistake and reroute any wrong turn and guide us in the direction of His beautiful ending. His plans and desires for us are always far better, far greater, than anything we might ever plan and desire ourselves. Our broken plans are just His better plans under construction. And this stone simply reminds me, He sometimes uses unexpected detours to take us there.

I suppose I should really tell you where our tram journey ended up that day. Only the best shopping centre in Prague. I kid you not. This detour made two young(ish) women from Belfast very happy. And what's better still; we visited the castle the next day too. That's a win-win if you ask me.

Looking at today's circumstances can leave us feeling confused. Looking ahead to tomorrow's unknowns can cripple us with fear. But looking back to God's faithfulness will help us face forward in faith. Never did I imagine I would sit alone in my two-storey, three-bedroom home and write a book about being single. Talk about an unexpected detour. And, right now, I have absolutely no idea how the words in my heart become words in your hand. But when I delve into my collection of stones, I am reminded that I can trust God. For He has never failed me yet. And, you can be sure, if you are reading these words today, you are holding one of the latest additions to my stone collection.

Sweet friend, this journey might not look as we expected, but God isn't about meeting our expectations. God is in the business of exceeding expectations. I have many stones to remind me of this truth. And something tells me, you will too. Our plans may still be broken, but His plans are always better. Unimaginably better. I guess, you don't need to know the plan, to know it's a good one.

Friend, buckle up. Let's see where this journey takes us. I have a stone collection that tells me it's going somewhere good.

CHAPTER 4

Undivided Attention, Undivided Strength

Recently I was driving to a friend's house when, surprisingly, I got lost. Talk about an embarrassing phone call because I should have known the way. It is just forty minutes away from my home. But forty-minute car journeys simply equal forty-minute live concerts, featuring me. Usually, I just wind the window down and crank the music up and before I know it, I arrive at their house. My final destination. Thank you very much Mr sat-nav-Creator-Man. You have made this girl's life a whole heap easier.

Hands down, sat navs are one of the greatest inventions of all time. Right up there with hair removal cream and those sucky-in, high-waisted pants. Girl, I know you get it. Those pants are woven together by angels themselves and hide all kinds of nasty.

Am I right? But sat navs; you just type in exactly where you want to go and voilà. Set your car to cruise control and follow that sweet-talking English accent all the way to your final destination. To the place you always wanted to end up. The place you always planned to end up.

But if your navigational skills are anything like mine, you will know that a sat nav is only as great as one of those heavenly stitched undergarments, when you remember to put it in your car. Which, on this particular day, I had not. Ugh. Panic overwhelmed me as I slid my hand down the side of my seat to discover my trusted English friend was not there. And I was already fifteen minutes into my journey. My head is such a sieve sometimes.

My sat-nav was lost and apparently, so was I. I studied my surroundings to see if anything looked familiar. Maybe a shop. Or a street name. Or a graffiti-filled wall with a catchy slogan plastered all over it. A landmark or a monument to remind me where I was and where I was going. But, no. I got nothing. Landmarks populated the landscape and monuments stood tall and embarrassingly obvious. But, somehow, I had always failed to notice them. Let's just say, I am a destination girl. I am not a journey girl.

And boy, do you miss a lot when you are a destination girl like me. I have to admit; the GPS of my single heart is often programmed to one destination too; my future. I think it is for many of us single girls. Single is where we are today and single is exactly where we don't want to be. We want out of here, and out of here ASAP. So, we programme our hearts, we set our minds and we fix our focus on future days. On better days.

But I wonder just how many things I miss *today* because I am so focused on my *one day*. I wonder how many life landmarks go by unseen, monumental opportunities pass by unexplored and precious, precious moments fly by unnoticed, simply because I am a destination girl and not a journey girl. Even today I had a conversation with God which went a little something like this: 'God, if you could just teach me everything I need to learn right now and really, really quickly, so I can move on from here, then that would be really, really great. Oh, and thank You. Amen'.

Ugh. It's hard when you feel stuck in a season you don't want to be in, for much longer than you'd like to be in it, isn't it? But any girl so set on getting onto the next season will miss getting the most out of this season. Mission-minded people can miss a lot of things.

Hearts fixed on future days can struggle to make sense of today's circumstances. Empty houses and unchecked boxes are hard for any single girl to make sense of. But those who simply wait for the promises of tomorrow can easily miss God's plans and purposes today. You see, God's definition of waiting is much different to ours. When I say, 'I am waiting for my one day', He responds, 'but I AM is working today'.

Take a moment to read that sentence again. When I say, 'I am waiting for my one day', He responds, 'but I AM is working today'.

Yes, He is certainly working today. If only we might switch our attention from our one-day dream destination and fix our focus on today's journey. I want to be a better journey girl. I need to be a better journey girl.

I just never realised how much until my twenty-ninth birthday. Officially 365 days away from jumping into the dizzy heights of the 30–40s age bracket and one step closer to joining that 'Knitting and Nattering' group I was talking about earlier. The big 3–0 was looming and wow, did that number feel huge to me. Still single. Just a whole lot older. Why not set fire to my hopes and dreams with the thirty candles on my birthday cake, for crying out loud?! But anyway, I'm over it now. Well, sort of.

On the run up to this milestone birthday, it hit me: I am a destination girl at heart. You see, shortly after the breakup, I rewrote my life goals, I reworked my timeline and I reset the co-ordinates of my heart once more. My circumstances had changed, but my dream had not. I still wanted to be married one day. I still do. So, with pure grit and determination, I fixed my focus on getting to my dream destination. Other things seemed less important. A lot more flexible. So, I placed these things on hold and decided I would revisit them once the marriage box was checked. This time just didn't seem like the right time, you know? I thought, I'll just sit back and wait. Wind the window down. Pump up the beats. Sing my soon-to-be-wed heart out and wait some more. Wait for my English friend to one day announce, 'You have arrived at your final destination. Mr Right is on your right. And have a nice wedding day.' Seriously, how handy would this invention be? Like, for real? I'll take two please.

Falling in love and getting married can so easily become a pivotal moment on which we pin all other life moments. Want to buy a house? *Maybe when I'm married.* Want to travel? *Hmm, maybe with a husband.* Want to change career? *Better leave that one too.* Want to start a ministry? *Someday, but not today.* And before you know it, the decisions you make and the steps you take and the plans you create today, somehow hinge around your one-day, but not-yet dream. And so you place life on hold, and you wait. For circumstances to change. To be better. For the right time. A better time. Which, for single destination girls like me, often involve a change in relationship status. A better one.

But on my twenty-ninth birthday I realised, I was waiting for my single days to pass by, while many significant life moments passed by me.

When I felt the gentle nudge of God to write this book, I agreed. In a my-mouth-says-yes-but my-heart-says-no kind of way. But I'll tell you more about that later. Anyway, I set my eyes on the end goal because that's what we destination girls do, right? We want the end product without the process. We want the final destination without the painfully long journey. Write the book. Release the book. Forget the book. And job done. I wish I could say this deep-rooted determination was because I could not wait for your precious fingers to flick through these pages. I really do. But deep down, I secretly hoped that once this book was finished, this season would be finished too. I mean, single author meets single publisher is just another Hallmark movie waiting to happen, right? Cue many, many hours sitting in front of a computer screen, frantically typing to get this book done. My brain can rationalise thoughts like this so easily. But now I am a couple of years into this book-writing process. Yes, years. A lot longer than I ever expected. A lot longer than I ever wanted. I have discovered God's plans for us always reach far beyond reaching any end goal.

Years of learning new ways are poured into these pages. Months of unlearning old ways spill over each sentence. And many, many days of relearning everything all over again flood every draft. This book-writing journey has been a difficult one to endure. But God knows the importance of this journey for me. And He knows the importance of this journey for you too. Whether it's navigating this single season, or maybe something else, God's plans always reach far beyond you reaching any end goal. And although this middle ground may feel uneven and uneasy, uncomfortable and unsettling, God loves us too much to bring us out of this season too early and He loves us too much to bring us into the next season too soon. He wants to use today to change us, challenge us, refine us, rework us, teach us, train us, prepare us and prune us. He wants to cut some old things off. Unhealthy thoughts and ugly attitudes and unproductive qualities. And create room for new things to grow and flourish and develop. And no amount of time spent frantically trying to hurry this process up will ever make Him move faster than what He knows is best.

Yes, God knows the importance of today for you and me. Because:

Today's attitudes become tomorrow's actions.
Today's thoughts become tomorrow's thought patterns.
Today's habits become tomorrow's habitual routines.
Today's learning becomes tomorrow's living.
Today's decisions become tomorrow's direction.
And today's direction becomes tomorrow's destination.

Friend, tomorrow's dream can become today's distraction if it remains the main focus. But God always sees incredible purpose in the journey. So what if, instead of waiting for God to finish

His work with us and take us straight to the beautiful ending He promises, we allow Him to complete His work in us today and show us beauty in the journey there too? What if, instead of altering our circumstances today, we allow God to alter us? What if, instead of changing our relationship status, we invite God to change our hearts' status? Certainly, God has unimaginably good plans for you and me. And it promises to be beautiful. But God has present plans for us too. Might these plans be beautiful too?

If I said Jeremiah 29 to you, your best guess of what might follow would probably be right. This verse is written on new job cards and new baby cards, graduation cards and 'I'm-so-sorry-for-your-breakup' cards. Yup. You've got it. Jeremiah 29:11:

> "'For I know the plans I have for you," declares the LORD, plans to prosper you and not to harm you, plans to give you hope and a future.'"

An incredible verse. A wonderful promise for the Jewish people in that moment of history. Here; God promised good plans, a wonderful future and a glorious hope for His people. He still does. But let's read this verse in the right context. A consequence of sin had left the Jews stranded on the shores of captivity and living as exiles in the land of Babylon. They were far, far away from the comfort and familiarity of home and thrust into a land plagued with all kinds of fear and uncertainty. They didn't want to be in Babylon. They wanted to be back in Judah. Let's just say, their Babylon is our Singleville, and they didn't want to be there for much longer either. And yet, God tells them to settle there. Why? Because the fulfilment of Jeremiah 29:11 would not be for another seventy years. Seventy years! That's a long time to be waiting and wanting and wishing and wondering, isn't it?

It could have been easy for the Jews to set the GPS of their hearts on Judah. Fix their focus on future days. On better days. Wait out those seventy years. Wait for future blessings. But God had different plans. Look at what He tells His people to do in just a few verses before:

'Build houses and live in them; plant gardens and eat their produce. Take wives and have sons and daughters; take wives for your sons, and give your daughters in marriage, that they may bear sons and daughters; multiply there, and do not decrease. But seek the welfare of the city where I have sent you into exile, and pray to the Lord on its behalf, for in its welfare you will find your welfare.'

JEREMIAH 29:5–7, ESV

Notice the words of instruction He uses. Build. Live. Plant. Eat. Take. Have. Give. Bear. Marry (and every single Jesus girl said amen). Multiply. Seek. Pray. Find.

Babylon was not some middle ground to be missed. A place to wait out present days and wait for future days. No, there was room for growth there. Opportunity for expansion. Plans for development. Potential for change. God did not want His people to constantly strive for Judah for those seventy years. Nor did He want His people to merely survive in Babylon for those seventy years. He wanted His people to live in Babylon, and thrive there too.

True to His word, God did bring His people back into Judah

exactly when He said He would. What a beautiful reminder to us today of the faithfulness of God. Friend, if He said it, He will do it. But don't miss the journey to it. A cheesy rhyme, but hey – who doesn't like a bit of cheese anyway? We have this assurance: if single is where we are today, then single is exactly where God wants us to be today. Now, I don't want you getting the wrong idea here. Overnight I did not suddenly develop the insatiable desire to remain single all my days. Not one bit. So I know how difficult it is for truth like this to translate into real life sometimes. Today, you might reach for a marker and highlight these words in your book. Underline each one. Fold down the corner of this page. Nod along in agreement. But when tomorrow comes and your status remains unchanged, these words are not so easy to hear. Days are still dateless. Nights are still lonely. Dreams are still distant. And breakups still hurt. But truth is truth no matter what day you read it. If single is where we are today, then single is exactly where God wants us to be today. Marriage is not a status God wants us to strive for. Single is not a status He wants us to just survive either. No, He wants us to live and thrive in whatever season we find ourselves in.

So, in the run up to my big... well, you know what age, I challenged myself to be a better journey girl. I wrote a list. A list of thirty things I wanted to do before my next birthday. See a Broadway show. Complete a physical challenge. Visit the Grand Canyon. Milk a cow. Eat a banana. I know, I know. Nearly thirty years on this Earth and I had avoided those bendy, yellow things. But they just look weird, OK. Anyway, where was I? Oh yes, the list.

Deep down, I knew this had absolutely nothing to do with anything written on a list and it had everything to do with the spiritual journey I was on. I mean, I don't want to over-spiritualise bananas, but sometimes it's good to do something in the physical to remind us of what God is teaching in the spiritual. This list was my reminder to stop waiting for *tomorrow* and start living *today*. To stop striving for the promises of *one day* and thrive in His plans and purposes *today*.

People say us singles have more time. I see their point. Right now, we don't have the responsibilities that come with being a wife. Our time is our time. But everyone gets the same amount of it. What we do with our time is what really matters. Busy social lives can help distract us from non-existent love lives. I get that. But busy social lives can also distract us from what's really important: our spiritual lives.

The Bible doesn't say much about singleness. But in 1 Corinthians 7, the author Paul, a fellow singleton, talks about the benefits of it. Pfft, I know right?! But let's listen to what he says:

'I would like you to be free from concern. An unmarried man is concerned about the Lord's affairs – how he can please the Lord. But a married man is concerned about the affairs of this world – how he can please his wife – and his interests are divided. An unmarried woman or virgin is concerned about the Lord's affairs: her aim is to be devoted to the Lord in both body and spirit. But a married woman is concerned about the affairs of this world – how she can please her husband. I am saying this for your own good, not to restrict you, but that you may live in a right way in undivided devotion to the Lord.'

1 CORINTHIANS 7:32–35

Can I be honest with you again? As I approached thirty, I realised I wasn't as unmarried as I thought. I was married. Just not in the sense I hoped. Instead, I was married to the idea of marriage. I was married to my dream. I wonder if you, too, have a single relationship status, but not a single heart status. For many years, my focus was fixed on finding a husband. My time was spent trying to reach my goal. My diary was spread across endless activities I thought would get me there, and get me there much quicker. The goal of marriage can distract our minds and consume our days so easily. But I don't want to live like this anymore. And I hope you don't either.

A woman who projects too far into the future can easily miss God's project right now. You see, although there are lots of things God wants to do in us today, there are lots of things He wants to do through us today too. *Build* someone up with encouragement. *Live* generously. *Plant* yourself in a church. *Take* time out to rest. *Give* your talents to an organisation. *Bear* with one another in love. *Seek* God's face. *Pray* for a neighbour. *Find* a new hobby. *Spend* time with those who help you, and those who need you too. *Improve* a skill or maybe *develop* a new one. *Grow* in faith. *Send* a kind text message. *Make* a phone call. *Write* a book about being single. Go crazy and *eat* one of those yellow, bendy things. *Find* one thing God wants you to do today, and just do it.

Every morning I wake up, I challenge myself to ask God for His perspective on the next 24 hours. Not tomorrow. Not next month. Not next year. But the day ahead. Then, I ask Him for His help. To fix my focus on what matters. To help me tune into my surroundings and maintain my attention. To be present in the present. Don't let the sweetness of this phrase run past you.

Allow it to rest in your soul today. Be present in the present. God certainly delights in the journey and oh, how I don't want to get to the end and realise how much good stuff I missed along the way. I don't want this middle ground to be missed ground. I want it to be memorable ground. I don't want this waiting season to be a wasted season. I want it to be God's time to work in and through me. And, something tells me, you do too.

Now, please hear me on this. Of course, it is not wrong to hope and dream and anticipate future days. It is right to make plans. It is good to be prepared. Focusing on today does not mean we neglect our futures altogether. But my point is this: we are not supposed to live there. In fact, we are not designed to live there.

Let me ask you a question: how often do you think about your future? The work meeting tomorrow. The first date next week. The conference next month. The holiday next year. The man you might marry. The house you might own. The kids you might raise. The life you might live. And so on, and so on, and so on. I think about my future a lot. With two feet and high hopes I jump into my tomorrows, only to helplessly flail around in the sea of unknown details and unanswerable questions. I drown in the depths of 'don't knows'. I am weighed down by the waves of 'what ifs'.

'What if something goes wrong…?'
'What if it doesn't go to plan…?'
'What if I never meet someone…?'
'What if I have this "gift" of singleness…?'
'What if I don't have kids…?'
'Or what if I can't have kids…?'

These questions grab my attention. They hold me captive and leave me wrestling worst-case scenarios. We do that, don't we? Our worst-case scenarios become our best-guess conclusions. One simple thought of tomorrow can lead us down such destructive paths sometimes. One thought leads onto the next, which leads onto the next. And before you know it, you pull hard on the brakes and disembark the thought train with baggage tagged 'worry', 'fear' and 'doubt'.

I am a perfect example of how to do this badly. Welcome aboard my crazy train of thought. It's chaotic, so please hold on tight. The other day I got to snuggle my friend's newborn baby boy. He's cute and tiny and smells brand-spanking new. But cuddling new babies often leave me cradling old fears. *Will I ever have a baby of my own? Guess I need to get a husband first. OK, so will I ever have a husband? Oh dear, I haven't had a date in months. Yikes. I am getting older now. Much older. Will it even be physically possible for me to have a baby? I know Sarah had one at ninety, but you know, that was Bible times. Biological clocks just don't tick the same these days.* A quick fast-forward through many years of first dates, failed dates and don't forget the menopause, and I somehow end up thinking about ninety-year-old me. Ninety-year-old me, sitting on my rocking chair. Ninety-year-old me, sitting and knitting on my rocking chair, because of course I joined the 'Knitting and Nattering' club. Ninety-year-old me, sitting and knitting, and most likely nattering, in a nursing home. All alone. No husband. No children. No grandchildren. No visitors.

Ugh. It's exhausting. And it doesn't take me long to get there either. I just draw a line from one imagined fear of tomorrow to where I am today, and I struggle to catch a breath. I do have a great imagination, but sometimes my imagination takes me to unimaginably bad places. Places I cannot survive. Places I cannot thrive.

Jesus knew this about me. And if you have ever followed your own train of thought and disembarked somewhere beyond the boundary of this 24-hour period, He knew this about you too. He knew we would think about our futures often. And it is in the context of future thinking that Jesus teaches His disciples about worry in Matthew 6. This is what He says:

'Therefore I tell you, do not worry about your life, what you will eat or drink; or about your body, what you will wear. Is not life more than food, and the body more than clothing? Look at the birds of the air; they do not sow or reap or store away in barns, and yet your heavenly Father feeds them. Are you not much more valuable than they? Can any one of you by worrying add a single hour to your life?

MATTHEW 6:25–27

'Therefore do not worry about tomorrow, for tomorrow will worry about itself. Each day has enough trouble of its own.'

MATTHEW 6:34

The word 'worry' here means *to be divided*. This makes a whole lot of sense to me. Worry divides. I know it, because I feel it. The pull in one hundred different directions and the stretch to a million different endings. You see, worry takes strength intended for today and spreads it amongst tomorrow's potential problems. It shares it across all possible outcomes. Realistic ones and unrealistic ones too. And when strength is stretched between today and tomorrow, it wears thin and it wears us out.

Worrying about tomorrow drains me. Waiting for tomorrow drains me too. But don't they often come hand in hand? The more we wait, the more we worry. The more we worry, the more strength we divide. And the more strength we divide, the less strength we have today. And I need a whole lot of strength if I'm going to survive some days, much less thrive.

I think that's why the enemy loves to hang out in waiting rooms. Our enemy is a predator who targets his prey at their point of weakness. And what is more vulnerable to attack than a worried woman who is weary from waiting? He knows waiting room chairs are uncomfortable. Of course, you can sit on them for a while, but as time goes on, muscles begin to ache. And in attempts to ease any discomfort, feet begin to wander and minds begin to wonder. Questions like 'What might happen next?' and 'Will it be good news?' and 'When will it be my turn?' relentlessly swirl around your mind. The quiet murmurs of others fill the otherwise silent room. Like a ticking clock, you tune into their words and struggle to avoid their conversations. Hopeful parents ask for updates on the love life. Tipsy relatives ask if you even like guys anymore. Well-intentioned friends encourage you to try online dating one more time. Maybe lower a standard or two. And unknowing strangers ask if you actually ever want to be married. Their words rub salt in the wounds of an already weary-from-waiting heart.

The enemy can so easily transform waiting rooms into worry

rooms. He only has to shift our focus from today and place it on tomorrow. That way, we are stretched and weakened and vulnerable to his attack. He knows we cannot survive today, much less thrive today, if we constantly strive for tomorrow.

Even Jesus Himself acknowledged each day is hard enough without adding tomorrow's trouble into the equation. He knows some days will be difficult and some seasons will be long. So, when Jesus teaches 'do not worry', He means this: don't divide the strength I promise to give you today with tomorrow's fears. Don't deplete yourself of the strength I will give you today by sharing it with tomorrow's uncertainties.

I like the way Eugene Peterson puts it:

'Give your entire attention to what is God is doing right now, and don't get worked up about what may or may not happen tomorrow. God will help you deal with whatever hard things come up when the time comes.'

MATTHEW 6:34, MSG

Sometimes we get so wrapped up in what we think God should be doing or wondering what He is going to do, that we miss what He is actually doing. Right here, right now. A disappointing relationship status can distract any girl's heart from what God is doing in this very moment. But God wants our attention today because He knows it's good for us. He sees the negative impact that dwelling on past days and striving for future days can have on us emotionally, physically, mentally and spiritually. So here's something I try to do every time my train of thought steams ahead to the next 24-hour period. Maybe you can try this too.

First, *recognise* when it's tomorrow's problem. When I worry about being single and my thoughts visit ninety-year-old Paula in the nursing home, I need to remind myself this is not today's problem. My guess is, a lot of your single-girl worries and fears are based on future days too. We need to stop the thought in its tracks before it stops us. Then, we must *remind* ourselves this worry is not ours to carry. Didn't Jesus command us not to pick up tomorrow's troubles? Instead, He instructs us to lay down every future fear, every pending problem, every coming concern, and place it before God, the only One strong enough to carry its weight. Then, we must *redirect* our focus to the day ahead. Ask God what He wants us to do in the next 24 hours. And then, *recalibrate* to His strength. The strength He promises to give us so we might achieve this. *Recognise. Remind. Redirect. Recalibrate.* And when today drifts into the past and tomorrow becomes the present, we *repeat* this same cycle all over again. *Recognise. Remind. Redirect. Recalibrate. Repeat.*

Friend, He promises us a good future, but we are not designed to live there. We are designed to live right here, right now. Undivided attention equals undivided strength to thrive today. Let's be better journey girls. Take our eyes off tomorrow's dreams, fears and everything in between, and carry the strength He promises to give us into the next 24 hours. Something tells me God is working. He always is.

CHAPTER 5

The Pandemic of Pace

Do you ever have just one of those weeks? OK, just so we are on the same page, try reading that sentence again. This time; dial in the perky and be a little more melodramatic. OK, go for it.

Do you ever have just one of those weeks? *Sigh.*

This was not a good week. Actually, that's not entirely true. It was a good week. It was a good, good week for many, many people. People I love. People I care about. People I truly want the best for. Happiness signposted every turn and good news painted every corner. I mean, not one, not two, but three, baby announcements flooded my Facebook. *Three.* And, of course, I liked every single one of them. That's got to count for something, right? Two of my close friends had babies and we all know how that goes. All aboard the crazy thought train all the way to the nursing home.

Yup, still knitting. Still no visitors. I know, I know. I'm supposed to stop the thought train before I dismount somewhere in my future, but some days I have to relearn this one all over again. Yesterday I received a text message from a good friend who got engaged. Now, I could prepare myself for the babies, but that one definitely caught me by surprise. But yay... for them. A few days ago I spent time with my family and guess what? Out of a family of seventeen first cousins, my one and only fellow singleton announced her brand-new love connection. Oh, and did I mention she is nearly half my age? She looked happy. I looked happy too. Smiles still mask a lot of hurt. I saw a photograph of an old boyfriend on social media. He was up some picturesque mountain with his new, picturesque girlfriend. They looked so in love and she looked so very beautiful. And skinny. Yes, much skinnier than me. And the wind seemed to catch her luscious, long hair at just the right angle to frame her freckle-free face. You know, one of those candid shots. Let's just say; candid and Paula are two words never used in the same sentence. I'm less can-did and more can't-didn't when it comes to unplanned photography. Anyway, I liked that picture too. I can be such a good Christian sometimes. And to top it all off, I just found out my 'back-up' is now in a relationship. How rude. It was like he didn't even know I had reserved him for later life if both of us remained unmarried. What am I supposed to do now? Maybe I should try online dating again? Or maybe I should do something crazy like change career, or possibly move country. Cast my net a little wider in this rapidly depleting sea of suitable singles. Decisions, decisions, decisions.

Sigh.

Yes, it was a good week. A confetti-cannon, glass-clinking, happy-cheering kind of week for many, many, *many* people. Which somehow made it a not-so-good week for me. This single business doesn't seem to get any easier, does it? Every announcement felt like a confetti cannon aimed straight for my single heart. Every celebration felt like a shard of glass tearing through my hopes and dreams. And every happy cheer provoked another hurting cry and slapped *single* straight across my can't-didn't, freckled face, all over again.

It's strange writing down my internal thoughts of this past week for you to read. It feels like I am sharing my best-kept secrets. Diary entries which expose parts of me I never want anyone to know are there. Moments when my finger hits 'like' but my heart holds hurt. Moments when my mouth cracks a smile but my heart breaks and cries. Moments when a picture-perfect photograph highlights all the negatives in me. But these are my struggles. My daily struggles. And, I suspect, these are your struggles too. We all have moments like this. Little moments dotted throughout our day that remind us we are still single and don't want to be. Little moments when comparison catches us off guard and insecurity invades our lives. Little moments when time seems to move so fast and life feels so very slow.

There was something so sweet-sounding about the year 2020. It literally oozed epicness. A year destined for perfect vision and incredible clarity and welcomed normalcy. And although I never verbalised it, anticipation filled my heart with what might lie in store for the next 366 days. Incredible, I thought. Even an extra day this year to make my dreams a reality. Exploding confetti consumed the room and enthusiastic cheers filled the air as the clock finally struck twelve. I don't like New Year's Eve much. Never really have. I mean, it is just another day. We stay up later than we're used to and eat more food than we're supposed to, only to count down the end of one day and welcome the beginning of another. Like every other single day gone before. And yet, something about this day drives many people to celebrate. The clock resets. This is a pivotal moment. The calendar renews. This is a defining moment. And the countdown restarts all over again.

My friend Vic and I hash-tagged this year 'the year of miracles'. We laughed and we joked, but hidden underneath our usual guise of humour, we were hopeful. I first met Vic a few years ago when a mutual friend introduced us at a large church event. Casual catch-ups quickly turned to awkward silences when this mutual friend asked if I was engaged yet. Awkward. Very awkward. She was sorry to hear about the breakup. I joked to fill the silence. But Vic, she understood exactly what my humour was hiding. A whole pile of hurt. In that moment, my breakups were a reflection of her own. Both recently single and both struggling with the aftermath of a curveball crisis. We didn't know it then, but this awkward introduction was the foundation of a solid friendship. One built on the common ground of broken dreams.

Still single and now in our thirties, we wondered if maybe, just maybe, 2020 would be the year where impossibilities turned into possibilities, improbabilities became probabilities and dates actually lived up to their name, and had dates. Maybe this would be the year; new year, new me, new last name.

People have always tried to reassure me that when my time finally comes, it will all happen quickly. Meet – engaged – married, all within a short timeframe. I think married people are told to say stuff like this to single girls like us. But hey, sign me up for that plan. So yes, year 2020 – I was hopeful. I was not prepared for the headlines. I don't think anyone was. No sooner had the confetti settled, was it brushed away again and completely forgotten about. Instead, death swept across the world at an unsettling rate and a new word entered the nation's vocabulary. COVID-19 was born. The once hopeful cheers turned to hurting cries, as nations mourned the loss of many, many lives. Unprecedented and unexpected. Streets once bursting with animation and energy and activity and life, turned eerily quiet, alarmingly dull and strangely slow. Unfamiliar and unusual.

This virus did not consult anyone's plans before it hijacked the year. It did not heed anyone's agenda or follow anyone's itinerary. Without warning, it settled in like an uninvited guest and caused havoc wherever it went, leaving behind only trails of destruction and devastation and disappointment. The usual routine of day-to-day life was interrupted by a virus that spread across the world like wildfire. Difficult to contain. Impossible to predict. Plans were derailed and dreams were diverted. Engagements were postponed and dates were rescheduled. Projects were cancelled and gatherings were dispersed.

And I sat at home, alone.

During the several months of 'lockdown' enforced across the United Kingdom, the fact I was still single was unavoidable. No busy schedule to distract from any discomfort of waiting. No fast pace of life to replace a love life on the go-slow. Empty diaries and vacant houses and one-person Zoom boxes will make any girl's single status painfully obvious. I guess God never got the memo of my new year, new name plans. I mean, dating is hard enough without making it unlawful to leave your house to see anyone. Am I right? Being alone is difficult enough without adding social distancing into the equation. Come on, God. Like, seriously?! Meeting someone seems downright impossible sometimes.

The brake pedal of my life, and many others, had been firmly pressed. Everything seemed as though placed on pause. And when the world stops, it's easy to see where you stand in comparison to others. It's easy to see where you stand in comparison to where you thought you would be too. During the COVID-19 pandemic, time quickened with each day that passed, and yet my life didn't. God didn't seem to quicken either. He seemed slow. Inactive, even. Another year with no new name meant I was falling behind my schedule. I wanted things to be better. I wanted things to move faster. I wanted things to change sooner.

So often we have calendars and clocks and countdowns in our minds, don't we? Targets we want to reach, and when we want to reach them. But when time elapses and targets remain untouched, we can feel right back at the beginning of this journey all over again. No broken arms. Just broken dreams.

A longing heart met with an unexpectedly long wait or uncomfortably deep want can be a tough journey to endure. But here's the good news; God is patient with us. He always accepts our broken pieces, no matter how many times we come back to Him with the same old shattered parts. He endlessly welcomes us to give Him our worries and our wants, our breakups and our breakthroughs. He lovingly invites us to share our deepest insecurities and our biggest fears with Him. He faithfully listens to our persistent prayers and repetitive requests. Over and over and over again. God is so patient with us. And for this, I am thankful. But He is also patient for us. He knows exactly where He wants us in the future and He knows exactly how to get us there. God is not slow. He is not late. Nor is He early. He is not delayed or distracted or deliberating what He might do next. He knows exactly what we need, exactly when we need it, to be exactly who He wants us to be, and go exactly where He wants us to go.

It took this global pandemic to point my single heart to another global pandemic of sorts. One that has been silently sifting its way through humankind for centuries. This pandemic, too, causes havoc wherever it goes and leaves behind only trails of destruction and devastation and disappointment.

The Pandemic of Pace.

Right now as you read these words today, I hope you know God has good plans for your life and have allowed this truth to settle deeply in your heart. But at this point in our conversation together, I feel so strongly I must expose the enemy. We must expose him, so he cannot impose himself on us. We must illuminate his ploys if we want to eliminate his power in our lives. Our enemy is a liar (John 8:44). And when truth does not settle in our hearts, his lies can unsettle us so easily. One of the more subtle lies the enemy has ever whispered to my single heart is this: *'Time is moving too fast and your life is moving too slow.'* The tick of any clock will put pressure on us girls to tick the next box, right? But there is a little verse tucked away in the book of Proverbs I want to show you. A verse to steady our hearts, and our feet, today. It says:

> 'In their hearts humans plan their course,
> but the LORD establishes their steps.'
>
> **PROVERBS 16:9**

The Hebrew word used for 'steps' here is *tsaad*, which also means pace. You see, God does not just establish the direction of our steps towards His beautiful ending, He sets the pace of our steps too. Many times, tears have trickled down my freckled cheeks as I have watched others follow a pattern of life I have not, cannot and will not be able to follow. Teardrops have gathered in the creases of my Bible as I have read and reread testimonies of others. All of which point to a God who is not bound by time like we are, but always delivers on His promise at exactly the right moment. I take comfort from stories like Sarah. God was not restricted by the ticking of her biological clock in the conception of Isaac (Gen. 21:2). I take hope from accounts like Joseph. God's promise was not delayed for thirteen years as he might have thought. Instead, the pit and the prison were vital entries in the timeline of his life which led to the promise of the palace (Gen. 50:20). These are real accounts of real people who spent real time waiting on God's promise. Don't let the simple flick of a page fool you. Every paragraph in their story is just a summary of days, weeks, months and years, filled with tears and turmoil, uncertainty and unknowns. Every full stop signifies a period in their life when God's time seemed off and His promise seemed slow. And yet today, we fast-forward to the end of their stories and conclude that, yes, God's timing is always right and His pace is always perfect.

When it comes to being single, I know what it's like for life to feel slow. Believe me. These days, first dates are like gold dust. Second dates are rarer still. And the clock just keeps tick, tick, ticking. We want things to be better. We want things to move faster. We want things to happen sooner. But the pace we keep today is so very important. His pace protects us. It prevents us from stepping into something too soon and it keeps us from reaching something too late. It stops us from falling. It keeps us from failing. It steadies us from fumbling. Yes, His pace protects us. His pace also positions us. It holds us where we need to be for exactly the right amount of time. It adjusts our steps today so we might tread exactly where He wants tomorrow. Yes, His pace positions us.

Time does not run away from God. Circumstances do not halt His purposes. Interruptions of life do not stop His promises. Other people's good news does not pause His good plans for us. No, His plans for all of us are good and each one is perfectly paced.

Here's something I've learnt recently; an altered pace equals an altered race. You see, if you go too slowly, you miss stuff. If you go too fast, you rush stuff. Our enemy knows this. He knows he can con us out of our promise, if he can simply compromise our pace. Our enemy knows he can divert us from God's good plan, if he can distract us or discourage us with the progress of others. This is the Pandemic of Pace. Our enemy knows he can steer us away from where God wants us to be, if he can entice us to strive for the position of others. This is the Pandemic of Pace. Our enemy knows he can prevent us from completing our God-assigned journey, if he can make us compete with the journey of others. This is the Pandemic of Pace. Our enemy knows he can stop us from being who God wants us to be, if he can drive us to imitate the role of others. This is the Pandemic of Pace. Our enemy knows he can keep us from reaching where God wants us to be tomorrow, if he can convince us to keep looking at our own calendars and clocks today. This is the Pandemic of Pace. Our enemy knows he can stop us from reaching God's beautiful ending, if he can debilitate us with decisions or freeze us in fear. This is the Pandemic of Pace. When the pace we keep is different from the pace God sets. The enemy wants to unsettle us so we *speed up*. The enemy wants to confuse us so we *stop*. The enemy wants to rattle us so we take *shortcuts*. Because an altered pace equals an altered race.

We live in a world that is driven by feelings. But when we follow our feelings, we adjust to all kinds of paces and end up in all kinds of unimaginably bad places. You see, frustration speeds up. Fear freezes. Hesitation trips up. Worry runs away. Doubt debilitates. Insecurity hides. Jealousy jumps into other people's lanes. Discontentment disables. Complacency settles. Covetousness chases. Impatience skips steps. All things that can, and will, alter our pace today if we allow. All things that can, and will, alter our race today if we allow. But faith, faith walks.

Keeping God's pace is not always easy, but it is essential. For a girl who remains in step with Him is a girl destined for His good plan for her life. And, sweet friend, what a threat this truly is. So, over the next few chapters, we are going to uncover some things that many of us single Jesus girls encounter daily. Things that can alter our pace if we allow. But first, let's ask the right question. How do we keep in step with Him? How do we make sure we stay on the right path, keep the right pace and continue in the direction of His beautiful plans?

Well, I guess I learnt this the hard way. Last year, I travelled 4,000 miles away from my home in Northern Ireland and headed for the beautiful sunshine state of Florida, USA. Let me explain, this was not a 'holiday' as such. I booked my ticket just three weeks before jetting off and not many people know this trip ever happened. I didn't tag myself in at the airport or post my usual pre-flight selfie. To those who did know of my whereabouts, this last-minute plane ticket purchase looked like spontaneity at its finest. Little did they know it was a cry for help, cleverly disguised as an impromptu 'vacay'. Back then, I had no words to wrap around the reason why I wanted far away from home. But now, a little further down the road, I realise the Pandemic of Pace had afflicted my life once again and I battled against a serious bout of contagious comparison and infectious insecurity. Still single. Still disappointed. I was an easy target.

Early symptoms emerged in work when a colleague showed me photographs of her gorgeous family on holiday. *I didn't think it was possible for real people to look so good in swimwear.* Symptoms slowly developed when I spotted a beautiful young family enjoying an afternoon stroll together. *Don't some people just seem to have it all?* Things worsened that evening when my clothes felt tighter and the scales went higher. *I could have sworn these jeans fitted last month.* And by the weekend, symptoms continued to manifest as I sat again in church, alone. *What is wrong with me? Why is the seat next to me still empty? Why is everyone else so much further ahead of me?* Dissatisfied by where I was. Disheartened by where

I was not. Desperate to be further ahead. I just couldn't catch a break, so I decided to catch a flight instead.

Of course, these feelings were not something I could drop off at the airport. Simply forget about with a dash of vitamin D or wash away with a splash in the pool. No, each one squeezed into my luggage and travelled to the other side of the world with me. Comparison crippled me. Insecurity impaired me. Jealousy jolted me. And questions overwhelmed me. *Maybe I'm not good enough? Pretty enough? Fashionable enough? Skinny enough? Funny enough? Smart enough? Successful enough? Maybe if I was more like her, I would be happily married by now? Maybe if I had a better job, better opportunities, more brains, less weight, more confidence, fewer freckles, then maybe my life would have turned out the way I always planned it would? Maybe then I would be further along the track by now?*

I disembarked the plane feeling more than just the effects of a long-haul flight. The Pandemic of Pace had taken its toll. I was weary. Tired of trying to catch up with the lives of other people. I was exhausted. Worn out from attempting to change what I thought I could in order to feel better about who I was and where I was. Physically burnt out. Mentally done in. Emotionally worked up. Spiritually run down. I gathered my luggage and headed for the exit.

I knew my lift would be waiting, and I was right. Just beyond the exit door, there he was again. My dad. He arrived in Florida just one week before I did. This time, he was not running towards my hospital bedside to see my broken bones. This time, he was waiting in the arrival lounge to welcome my broken heart again.

Delight radiated his face as I slowly walked towards him. Just me and my luggage. As I drew closer, I noticed he grasped something tight in both hands. I guess, I got my Hallmark movie moment after all. Because clutched between his whitened fingers was an embarrassingly large piece of paper with my name handwritten on it.

I think my dad's handwritten words captured the whispers of heaven that day. God was waiting for me to come to Him. God was waiting for me to come to Him *again*. He was standing in position. Ready to embrace. Smile on His face. With hands holding a huge piece of card with my name beautifully written on it. A name He had chosen for me. A name He lovingly called me. The love of the Father enveloped me, as my dad squeezed me tight. And then I realised something; in efforts to run away from home, I ran straight to it. I was home. In my father's arms, I was home.

You see, home is not just a building. Home is that place where you find shelter and comfort, security and protection. That safe space. A haven. A place where you find rest from running and stillness from striving, quiet from questions and bandages for breakups. Home is where your deepest longings are fulfilled and your greatest needs are met. Where you experience belonging, sense genuine connection and know the meaning of real relationship. That place where you are called by name. Known by name. Given your name. The trouble today is, many people, not just singles, are searching the world to satisfy cravings that can only be met in constant connection and relationship with God. Searching for something that can only be found at home in the Father's arms.

During the COVID-19 pandemic, experts told us to stay at home. In a spiritual sense, I think the same advice is true for us today. We must find our identity, our contentment, our security, at home with God, before we venture into the world.

Friend, the Pandemic of Pace will make us want to run ahead of God, if not run away altogether, unless we learn to adjust to a different rhythm. His rhythm. In the airport foyer, once again my hurting heart felt the love of father. But more than just his heart. His heartbeat. Did you know that a typical human heart beats up to 100 times a minute? And did you know that an average human typically completes 100 steps a minute? That's one step per heartbeat.

Step.

Ba bum.

Step.

Ba bum.

Step.

Ba bum.

Each step in time with a typical heartbeat. Steady pace. Regular rhythm.

As we journey this middle ground together, faith indeed walks. And each step of our journey is perfectly paced with the heartbeat of our Heavenly Father. With proximity comes His pace. With relationship comes His rhythm.

Yes, the Christian life is a race. But God never asks us to race for Him, before He asks us to remain in Him (John 15:4). God never asks us to run for Him, before He asks us to run to Him. God never asks us to move forward, before He asks us to move closer. God never asks us to step again, before He asks us to be still. God never asks us to push ahead, before He asks us to press in. Each step of your journey is paced by God. And each step is set to the rhythm of constant relationship with Him. Deep connection between the Creator and His creation has always been God's Plan A.

In a world where the human race races, us single Jesus girls can struggle to keep a faith that walks. Some days are disappointingly dull and some seasons are so very slow. But the enemy can alter our race if he can alter our pace. He wants us to contend for contentment by chasing after the world's standards. To seek satisfaction by trying to change our relationship status. To jump from relationship to relationship and recklessly run into wrong ones. To stop waiting for God's time and skip important steps. To strive for more. Maybe even settle for less. Every day, words will bombard us, labels will try to stick to us, opinions will attempt to inform us and lies will seek to convince us, that time is moving too fast and our lives are moving too slow. This is the world's view. Not God's view.

The Pandemic of Pace is the underlying current that drives dissatisfied hearts to strive for bigger and better and faster and sooner. And yet, real relationship with the Father is the only thing able to satisfy any heart's craving. It's His love alone that can fill us. It's His sufficiency alone that can satisfy and sustain us. I know this to be true, because I've experienced it to be true. Today, as I write these words, the world continues to fight against one pandemic yet remains blinded to the other. Right now, I can't jump on a plane and run away to Florida, but I can choose to remain in Him. I do choose to remain in Him. This is a daily decision. A decision to keep an unbroken relationship with God. To take my eyes off the clock, the calendar, the countdown and the company that surrounds me, and to regulate my life with His rhythm. To pace my steps with His heartbeat.

In Hebrews 12, we are reminded to ' run with perseverance the race marked out for us, fixing our eyes on Jesus, the pioneer and perfecter of faith' (vv1–2). He is our pace-setter today. Certainly, there will be days He will want you to run. Get up and go after that dream. Take on that new challenge. Jump at that next opportunity. If His heartbeat quickens, you quicken. This is the rhythm of relationship. And then, there will be other days He will want you to stop. Wait for a while. Slow down. Be still. Sit on the sidelines and celebrate someone else's good news. If His heartbeat slows, you slow. This is the rhythm of relationship. So today, if we want to keep in step with Him and continue in the direction of His beautiful ending, we have to stay close to Him. And close enough to hear His heartbeat.

I wonder what this might look like for you today. Maybe it's breakfast in bed with your Bible or a daily devotional over dinner. Your identity and purpose is woven into its very pages. Maybe it's conversations with God over morning coffee or moments of stillness over supper at night. Daily dialogue with Him will help you discover His plans for each day. Maybe it's commutes to work in silence or walks in the park to pray. His words of instruction are heard in moments of intimacy with Him. Maybe it's studying scripture before scrolling social media or listening to online sermons before listening to the opinions of others. His words, not theirs, will fulfil your deepest longings. His presence, not their approval, will meet your greatest needs. Or maybe it's the embrace of a father, 4,000 miles away from home in an airport foyer. Deep relationship between Father and child is the heartbeat of Heaven. This is the heartbeat of home.

Every day, He wants us to come to Him with any luggage we might carry, tagged with labels of 'unwelcome', 'unpretty', 'unlovable', 'unwanted', 'unsuccessful'. And instead, He holds a huge piece of card with your name, my name, beautifully written all over it. A card that reminds us exactly who we are each day. Accepted. Beautiful. Loved. Chosen. Singled out. A card that reminds us exactly whose we are today. His child.

OK, so maybe the year 2020 didn't quite work out as I planned. No new-year-new-name for me. But today is a new day. And I choose to remain close to Him, so I can remain in step with Him. His plans are taking me somewhere good and I don't want to miss it. You won't want to miss it either.

So today, and every day, I hope you choose to do the same.

CHAPTER 6

The Confusion with Comparison

Cross-country running. No two words has this schoolgirl ever hated more. Well, that alongside Pythagoras' Theorem. These two words had the potential to wipe any smile off my youthful face and ruin any given day. Let me tell you, I am not a runner. Not then. Not now. Not ever. I'm the kind of girl who remains inactive in my activewear. I count walking to the fridge as cardio and shovelling a heaped fork of delicious food into my mouth as weightlifting. My imagination runs wild. My legs do not. Fact. But I do not like to lose. Also a fact.

My competitive nature dragged me around the track and urged me to finish the race, just like everyone else. I completed each lap with the kind of pace that says, 'OK, I'm not going for gold, but I am not finishing last. No way am I finishing last'. Determined, but realistic. Seasoned runners crossed the finish line long before I ever reached my final lap. They bypassed me with the grace of a gazelle, the speed of a cheetah and the stamina of an antelope. I swear, some girls sweat beads of glitter. And can talk and run all at the same time. Madness.

With every stride, my foot pounded the gravel with the elegance of a baby elephant and the pace and stamina of a non-athletic human. One who very much liked fast food and didn't have fast feet. No glitter. Just sweat. Like a mirage in the distance, the end was finally in view. One final loop around the track and I would cross the finish line at last. I spotted a friend not too far ahead and suddenly, something changed. No longer was the finish line my target. She was. I thought, 'If only I could catch up with her, then I would be happy.' I quickened my pace and before I knew it, we ran side-by-side in tandem. I glanced at her. She smiled at me. But who were we kidding? We both meant business. And we both knew it. We most certainly did. With one eye on the finish line, the other on the competition, it was time to go for it. My feet gained momentum as she gradually gained ground. The end was in sight, but my sight was no longer on the end. Oh no. My sight was on her. And any girl determined to catch up with another will eventually be caught out.

I certainly was. I never crossed the finish line that day. Let's just say my brain moved faster than my body could keep up and I plummeted to the ground just short of the end. Embarrassing moments have such as special way of finding me. But I just wanted to be where she was, if not slightly further ahead. So, I strived to keep a pace I was never designed to keep, and I fell. I fell hard.

You will know as well as I do, that this problem is not just reserved for schoolgirls in schoolyards. No. This is something many of us single Jesus girls encounter every day too. One eye on God's goal. One eye on the other girl.

I wonder who this 'other girl' is for you? It changes for me. Last week, it was the friend who got engaged. My cousin. The new mummies. My ex-boyfriend's new girlfriend with the skinny waist and flawless hair. I commanded my thumbs, and my mouth, to respond with words my heart fought hard to accept. 'I am so happy for you...'. A well-rehearsed script I use often. Each word predicted the next as my go-to reply seemed to write itself. Yesterday, it was a girl with no name. A fellow writer who won a competition I, too, entered. I bossed my feelings to celebrate her success, but my heart resisted the same instruction. The spotlight on her achievement seemed to cast a dark shadow over my attempt, only to reveal any feelings of failure my heart tried so hard to conceal. And looking ahead to my tomorrows, as I stare at yet another wedding invitation on my fridge. The one with a single name, my name, written on the spacious, dotted line. I can already predict who it will be that day too. Seriously. Like I need another reason to eat.

Some days, it's the girl with the chiselled abs. The dream job. The successful book. Other days, it's the girl with the perfect family. The long list of friends. The epic dating life. Scrap that, the existent dating life. Someone further along the track. Someone closer to the goal. Someone crossing into their dream while we are clutching for something that resembles ours. All from one simple text message. One announcement. One social media post. One rejection letter. One wedding invitation.

Let's face it. Some days it is easy to pace your steps with the heartbeat of God. But other days, you will scroll through social media and suddenly feel lonely again. You will hear of someone else's good news and suddenly feel left out again. You will have another run of bad dates or another month of no dates and suddenly feel disappointed again. You see what she has, and you want it. You see where she is, and you want to be there too. Comparison can nudge its way into our lives so easily and compel us to strive after. Hurry up. Move faster. Try harder. Push more. Wait less. In times like this, Jesus is no longer our pace-setter. She is. Our feet gain momentum. Our heartbeat quickens. And before we know it, we are face down in a pile of gravel. Bruised hands, bruised heart. Altered pace, altered race. You see, Satan will tap into our worry only to tempt us to hurry. And we can miss a whole bunch and mess up a whole lot when we try to hurry, right?

Comparison has caught me off guard many times throughout my life. From spelling tests in primary school to exam results in university. Pocket money in childhood to payslips in adulthood. Height measurements in younger days to hip measurements in recent days. Comparison is not something we grow out of, it just grows up with us. Subtly embedded in the rhythm of society, comparison accelerates the current that drives many to strive for bigger and better and faster and sooner. And us single Jesus girls can get swept away in this current so easily. Anyone can.

Just the other day, I had breakfast with one of my closest friends. Now, this friend is in a relationship and has been for many years now. Let's just say, when it comes to life goals, she seems well ahead of me. But having spent the day before with three of her other close friends, it was obvious she, too, was struggling.

Instead of a girlie catch up and carefree lunch, my friend spent the afternoon fourth-wheeling some mummy talk about 'boo-boos' and 'doo-doos'. Yes, she has a relationship. She seems so far ahead of me. But she doesn't yet have children. She seems so far behind them. Both of us, grading our position by the position of others. Measuring our success by meeting certain milestones. Calculating our progress by adding the number of boxes left unchecked on our to-do list of life. Both of us, full up on caffeine and knee-deep in comparison. And comparison is simply a spectator sport that nobody ever wins.

You see, comparison will often leave you feeling one of two ways. One: you will feel pretty good about yourself. *I'm just glad I am not where they are.* Or two: you will feel a whole lot worse about yourself. *I just wish I was where they are right now.* One results in pride. The other results in jealousy or insecurity. All crippling side-effects of the same comparison issue. Just opposite sides of the same comparison coin.

Many of us single girls are tricked to believe that once we find love, our comparison cravings will be satisfied at last. But a change of relationship status will never change the status of a comparison-crippled heart. Think about it. The single girl wants to be the married girl. The married girl wants to be the pregnant girl. The mummy of one wants to be the mummy of two. The girl on the sofa wants to be the girl on the plane. The girl in the mirror wants to be the girl in the magazine. The girl in the pew wants to be the girl on the platform. And so on, and so on, and so on. Comparison is not a circumstance issue. It's a heart issue. And a change of circumstance will only temporarily mask the comparison-crippled condition of any girl's heart.

It's hard not to compare with others. I get it. I really do. So, what if I told you comparison isn't wrong? Now stay with me on this one. I know this may seem to go against every piece of advice you have even been given, but let me ask you a question. How many times has someone told you not to compare, and you were able to do it? Me neither, friend. Me neither. You see, experience tells me comparison is unavoidable. After all, we are all different. We are all at different ages, different stages, of life. Every person who has ever lived and will ever live has their own individual journey to embrace. Different track. Different race. Different pace. Each day, our lives align with the lives of so many others. Our tracks run alongside the tracks of others. Think about it. We rub shoulders in the shops. We share coffee in the office. We pass smiles in the street. We shake hands in church. We share love on social media. Our lives run parallel *with* one another and yet, we are often told not to draw parallels *to* one another. Like this is something we should find so easy to do. But comparison is inevitable because differences are evident. To tell humans not to compare is to tell humans to ignore the very thing God created us to be. Different. Unique. One of a kind. Singled out. God infused diversity into the very DNA of mankind. His creativity is captured in variety. His imagination is gloriously displayed in every single person who has, and will ever be. Different skin colours and hair colours, different heights and weights, different personalities and talents and abilities to run and talk at the same time. You get the idea. We were intentionally created to be individual, not carbon-copies of one another.

For too long, I have tried not to compare and failed miserably. I simply cannot put blinkers on and pretend that differences do not exist and comparisons cannot be made, when every day I live on Earth I am reminded the opposite is true. So here's what I think: comparison is not the real problem. Why we do it, and what we do with it, however, is. I think we need a perspective shift. So right now, instead of telling you 'don't compare… it's wrong', I'm suggesting 'do compare… just do it right'.

But before we can learn how to compare right, we must first set our hearts right. A shift in attitude will help shape our actions. There is a story woven into three of the gospels I want to share with you as we tackle this together. A story about a man named Jairus.

'When Jesus had again crossed over by boat to the other side of the lake, a large crowd gathered round him while he was by the lake. Then one of the synagogue leaders, named Jairus, came, and when he saw Jesus, he fell at his feet. He pleaded earnestly with him, "My little daughter is dying. Please come and put your hands on her so that she will be healed and live." So Jesus went with him.'

MARK 5:21–24

Can you imagine how Jairus would have felt when Jesus agreed to go and see his little girl? The rush of relief. The surge of calm. The flood of assurance. But as Jairus and Jesus embark on their journey together, another story begins to unfold and weave its way into the narrative.

'And a woman was there who had been subject to bleeding for twelve years. She had suffered a great deal under the care of many doctors and had spent all she had, yet instead of getting better she grew worse. When she heard about Jesus, she came up behind him in the crowd and touched his cloak, because she thought, "If I just touch his clothes, I will be healed." Immediately her bleeding stopped and she felt in her body that she was freed from her suffering.

'At once Jesus realised that power had gone out from him. He turned round in the crowd and asked, "Who touched my clothes?" ...

'Then the woman, knowing what had happened to her, came and fell at his feet and, trembling with fear, told him the whole truth. He said to her, "Daughter, your faith has healed you. Go in peace and be freed from your suffering."

'While Jesus was still speaking, some people came from the house of Jairus, the synagogue leader. "Your daughter is dead," they said. "Why bother the teacher anymore?"'

MARK 5:25–30, 33–35

Notice how these two separate stories somehow collide and merge into one.

One named man. One unnamed woman.
Jairus asks and Jesus goes. The woman takes and Jesus stops.

And as a result, his daughter dies and this woman lives.

We can often read familiar stories like this and rush ahead to the ending we know is to come. But for a moment, let's pause and put ourselves in Jairus' shoes. Or sandals. Or whatever footwear synagogue leaders wore in those days. How might Jairus have felt in those middle moments? Although some details we are never told, the unwritten parts of the script allow us to place ourselves directly into the story. How might you have felt? Jesus stops to help this woman and this stops Jesus helping his little girl. How very unfair, right?

Many times along my journey, the same thoughts have swirled around my mind. These may not have been Jairus' thoughts. But they certainly are mine. A few months ago when someone in my world announced her engagement, hidden behind my cordial congratulations I silently calculated all the reasons why this should have been me and not her. I mean, *I* am the one who asked. She didn't even want a relationship and now she gets a ring. And a nice one at that too. How unfair. I reasoned; *I* am the one serving in church. *I* am the one reading and praying most days. Within a matter of moments of hearing her good news, I questioned her life choices. I pinpointed her character flaws. Even doubted if she followed Jesus at all. In doing so, I tried to tip the scales in my favour. I bigged myself up as more deserving. I belittled her as less deserving. How unfair that she gets and I don't. How unfair that she is happy and I am still hurting. I can justify my feelings and rationalise my arguments so easily. But this is not a one-time example. Oh, how I wish it was. This is an unhealthy pattern, which makes this a serious problem. Although on the surface, comparison seems to be the issue here, it's not. A critical heart condition is.

Here is something I have learnt over the last few years; sometimes we hurt not because of our current circumstance, but because of our current condition. Pain can often be an indicator, an alarm bell, to alert us to something, somewhere, that isn't right and needs our attention. Remember in Chapter Two when we talked about how God cares about our pain? This is true. God does care about our pain. But sometimes He will use pain to pinpoint areas in our lives that are unhealthy and that He wants to work through with us. Time may reveal pain, but it also reveals pain points. Unhealthy areas that need our attention. Unhealthy areas that need addressing. God is interested in our prognosis, not sticky plaster treatments or relationship upgrades that will only temporarily soothe a hurting heart. God is invested in developing us. Improving us. Bettering us. Digging below surface level issues and uncovering deep-rooted problems. Healing those broken parts to reveal more beautiful hearts. Truth is, there is little long-term value if your relationship status changes today but an unhealthy heart status does not.

As I have attempted to navigate this single season, God has uncovered many unhealthy heart issues in me. Ugly heart issues. I share this with you, not because it is easy or pretty. But because silencing the truth helps no one. We have walked through these pages together and although we might never meet in person, I consider you a friend. And I so desperately want to help you. Comparison is not the problem. There is often an underlying heart condition that is. One that causes us to respond to comparison in an unhealthy way. An ugly way. When I looked at my own heart, I discovered what was really going on. Jealousy. Anger. Bitterness. Envy. Discontent. Pride. And misdiagnosis of ourselves will often lead to the mistreatment of others. Jealous hearts will jump into her lane. Angry hearts react in haste. Bitter hearts spew words of hate. Envious hearts rejoice in her misfortune. Dissatisfied hearts constantly grab for more. Proud hearts disregard the position of others. Each attitude a sin. A stumbling block that affects not only us, but others too.

When we come to God with our hearts, we must learn to accept the help He chooses to give and trust that whatever He does, He does for our good. Our long-term good. God loves us too much to bypass unhealthy heart issues. He knows the good, the bad and the downright ugly, often hidden, parts of us that others do not see. He knows us so intimately, for He created us individually. So, I challenge myself, like King David, to pray these words. And today, I lovingly challenge you too:

'God, I invite your searching gaze into my heart. Examine me through and through; find out everything that may be hidden within me. Put me to the test and sift through all my anxious cares. See if there is any path of pain I'm walking on, and lead me back to your glorious, everlasting way—the path that brings me back to you.'

PSALM 139:23–24, TPT

Certainly, *look around*. God gifted mankind with peripheral vision to see vibrant variation and beautiful contrasts in the world, and each other. So, when you look around and notice the differences that are there, remember every race and every pace is designed to be that way. But don't stop there. Look around, then *look up*. Remember God has outlined a race only you can run. And then, commit to *look in*. Allow God to identify any heart condition that needs His loving care and attention. Surrender to His healing process. Invite Him to work with you, to work on you.

When I fixed my focus on God, I suddenly realised my friend's good news did not diminish God's good plans for me. Jairus found this to be true too. His story didn't end with the woman's success. And your story doesn't end with her success either. It's true, in human terms Jesus was too late for Jairus. But in God's terms, Jesus was right on time. How beautiful to know that His steps were perfectly paced for both Jairus and the unnamed woman to receive their miracle. It wasn't one first, the other last. One gets, the other goes without. One favoured, the other forgotten. When Jesus stops to help the woman, it doesn't stop him helping Jairus. In fact, the opposite is true. This 'delay' sets Jairus up for his miracle. An even greater miracle of resurrecting power which would see his little girl live again.

Right now, whether you are twelve years old or twelve years sick or twelve years single, His steps for you are paced so you can obtain His perfect plans for your life. His pace for her does not interfere with His pace for you. His provision for her does not limit His provision for you. His plan for her does not thwart His plan for you. His help for her does not hinder His help for you. The story of Jairus and the unnamed woman is just one incredible example of how God can masterfully coordinate and intertwine the lives of two individuals and orchestrate His perfect plan for both. When I grasp hold of this truth with two hands, suddenly comparison does not have the same hold on me.

Let's flip the script
Over the next 24-hour period, comparison will nudge its way into our lives one way or another. But how we respond to comparison

is our choice. I want to choose better. Instead of allowing my usual, unhealthy internal chatter to narrate my day, I choose to flip the script. So here are a few things for us to remember the next time the text message comes, the social media post uploads, the rejection letter arrives or the wedding invitation on the fridge catches our eye when all we want is a snack:

I will choose to complete, not compete
Wanting to be the best is something buried so deeply inside of me. I never verbalise it, but victims rarely do. And I don't think I am alone. Many of us grow up wanting to achieve the best grades. Obtain the best job. Get the best boyfriend. We want to be the smartest, the hottest, the skinniest, the funniest, the strongest, the fastest, the happiest. If not the best, at least better than her. But when we allow comparison to drive us to compete against one another, we compromise completing our race altogether. Here's what I've learnt. When comparison creeps into my day and tries to convince me to compete against someone else, I must ask myself these questions: Do I want to be better than her, or do I want God's best plans for me? One wants to be the best. The other wants God's best. Do I want to impress her, or do I want to leave an impression on her? One wants to be better than her. The other wants to leave her better.

Remember in Hebrews 12, when the writer reminds us to 'run with perseverance the race marked out for us, fixing our eyes on Jesus, the pioneer and perfecter of faith' (vv1–2)? Notice, *'the race marked out for us'*. God has a different path for each one of us to tread. His very best path. And it promises to be good. So, when happy news clogs my newsfeed and celebratory cheers reach my ears, I have a moment of opportunity to catch comparison before it catches me out. A swift moment to choose; will I allow comparison to urge me to compete, or will I fix my focus on the race only I can complete?

It's easy to get waylaid when constantly looking at other people's lanes. But the sidelines of someone else's journey is a sad and lonely place for any girl to sit. We each have our own race to run. We are aligned with others, not against others. Sweet friend, take notice of where God has placed you today. This is not a mistake. A mishap. An oversight. This is the intentional move of your very intentional God. The race He has outlined for you is as unique as you are. Singled out since the beginning of time. Your race is not hers. Her race is not yours. Neither is better. Neither is worse. They are just different. Equally good, because God is good. He does not run out of resources. We do not have to fight each other to win His favour. His blessings are not in short supply. We do not have to be the best to be blessed. God is good, and He is good to us. All of us.

I will choose to celebrate with her, not criticise her

I struggle to celebrate with others sometimes. My words will never say it, my actions will never show it, but deep down in my heart, I know it. Somewhere along my journey, I accepted this lie: there are only so many wins to go around. Which means, when she wins, I lose. Simple maths, right?

But a content heart will celebrate others, not criticise others. You see, contentment satisfies any comparison craving by reminding us of what we already have. When I look back over my life, I see God's goodness saturating my years. But God's blessings to me are a lot harder to see when I'm focused on His blessings to her.

No matter how many times I read the story of the Prodigal Son in Luke 15, I am always captivated by the older brother. I am shocked by his reaction. To criticise his younger brother and complain to his father, rather than celebrate his lost brother's return. I know his reaction is wrong. But I acknowledge his reaction is real. A real reaction from someone with a real problem. Much like me. Jealousy and pride can cloud our vision to the point we can no longer see the Father's goodness to us. In essence, the older brother had no right to complain. Everything his father had was now his. But sinful attitudes can narrow our focus and we can struggle to see God's blessings beyond the plank in our own eye sometimes.

We must choose a different response. A better response. When comparison comes, we can choose to thank God for His blessings in that moment. The warm cup of coffee in our hands. The friend who lives down the street. The food in the fridge, not the wedding invitation on it. You may not have exactly what you want. I know, some days I see what I don't have too. But don't allow what you don't have to prevent you from seeing what you do have. Notice His blessings. If right now you are struggling to do this, you should have a collection of stones to help remind you. And girls cannot gather stones and throw stones at each other at the same time.

A heart bursting with thankfulness will struggle to contain criticism. There just isn't enough room for both to co-exist. So, after you finish thanking God for His innumerable blessings to you, you are better positioned to thank God for blessing her too. When she wins, you don't lose. This is the world's way of thinking. In the body of Christ, when she wins, you win too. When thankfulness is the soundtrack of your day, suddenly the sound of her success doesn't seem so bad after all.

I will choose to complement her, not copy her

Have you ever tried to play the part of someone else? I have. Many years ago, I auditioned to be an extra in a movie. Ad read this: 'Seeking Quirky, Pale People For Hollywood Blockbuster Movie'. I signed up. One part of me excited by the prospect of being on a real-life movie set. The other part of me secretly hoping I would not qualify as 'quirky'. But, of course, roll out the red carpet. Quirky, pale woman living in Belfast plays quirky pale woman living underground. Isn't that just fantastic and a major boost of confidence? Anyway, a couple of months after my acting debut, I received another call. The agency had another role for me to play. I held my breath. And prayed for something a little more glamorous. Someone who lived above ground at least. But no. This time, the role declared as 'perfect for me' wasn't even living. A dead cavewoman. I kid you not. If quirky and pale wasn't enough, 'dead cavewoman' would surely tip any girl over the edge. Honestly, I am not an actress. But boy, will I try to copy others.

In the real world, acting the part of someone else is difficult to maintain. Accompanying someone else; now this is something we can do. Friend, it is possible to acknowledge there are differences, without adjusting to these differences. If God wanted me to have lovely, golden skin and less quirky facial features, He would have designed me that way. Believe me, I've talked to Him about this and I'm yet to wake up looking any different. Instead He created each one of us differently so we might accompany each other in life, not act like each other through life.

Have you ever listened to someone singing the harmony, without hearing the melody? It's awful. Believe me. There's nothing my family loves more than to gather together and belt out Disney classics and *Greatest Showman* hits. But even the high ceilings and great kitchen acoustics can't fix our problem. Yes, we sing loud and we sing proud, but we don't always sing in tune. You see, we attempt to harmonise with each other. We really do. But instead, we all copy each other. Everyone sings the harmony. Well, sort of. And no one sings the melody. And even the most beautiful harmony is incomplete without a melody. Same goes with us.

Here's the thing; if you choose to copy someone else, the world will miss your melody. There are notes only you can sing. These are not just nice words. This is truth. Before you were born, God penned lyrics only you could live and He composed a melody only you could master. That's what it means to be singled out. But God's masterpiece extends so far beyond any individual. It's often hard for human hearts to grasp how God can so deeply care for the one, while at the same time, so deeply care for the many. But that's what He does. Your lifesong is designed to bring the best out in hers. Her lifesong is designed to bring the best out in yours. Yes. God cleverly coordinates and masterfully intertwines every individual life so that He might orchestrate His overall perfect plan. For us all.

Now let me be clear, imitation in itself is not wrong. In fact, Paul instructs his readers to imitate him. To follow his example. To copy his way of life. But notice exactly what Paul says: 'Be imitators of me, as I am of Christ' (1 Cor. 11:1, ESV). Here's something to ask yourself when comparison compels you to copy someone else: Am I imitating her or am I imitating Jesus in her? There is difference. One makes you want to be better than her. The other makes you want to be a better version of you.

I have an amazing friend called Nichola. I'm pretty sure if angels wear bright, yellow raincoats and funky shoes, this girl is one. On my thirtieth birthday, Nichola treated me to a fun-filled day packed with activity and adventure. A pedicure. A spa. Followed by some afternoon tea. And after she settled the bill, she thanked me for allowing her to celebrate with me. She thanked me. *Me.* Hands down, Nichola is one of the kindest, most generous people I know. Her open hands and open heart are a true reflection of Jesus. I want to be like that. Not because I want to be more like Nichola. But because I want to be more like Jesus. The goal of any Christian is to become more like Him. But how often does comparison captivate us and compel us to copy things like hairstyles, clothes, body shape, job titles, relationship goals. Temporary things that have no eternal value.

Instead, we can choose to see Jesus in her. Every person is made in His image (Gen. 1:26). His imagination differentiates us, but His image connects us. God does not want us to be clones of one another. He wants you to be you, and me to be me. But God does want us to become more like Christ. He wants you to be the best version of you, and me the best version of me. To mirror His kindness. His love. His goodness. His patience. His peace. When we choose to copy Christ, we will complement each other. And He is glorified in and through both.

I will learn from the cloud and listen to the right crowd

The first part of a marathon is easy. Or, so I am told anyway. Every runner poised at the white line, ready to begin their race. Can you imagine standing in your position? The shotgun fires or the whistle sounds and you begin to run. Filled with excitement and anticipation of the next 26.2 miles. (Honestly, that number alone makes me sweat. Still no glitter!) The supporters are many and their enthusiastic cheers carry you for miles. But then you reach mile fifteen. Mile sixteen. Mile seventeen. Your energy dwindles, your legs ache and your feet begin to throb. And talk about the chafing. Vaseline, please. Here, the supporters are few and their cheers are faint. At this point, you have run a long way, but the finish line is still a long way off. Nowhere near the start. Nowhere near the end. Just somewhere in-between. It's true. People cheer for you at the beginning. People celebrate with you at the end. But what about the middle miles? What about the middle moments?

This is when runners really struggle. And this is when we often struggle too. The space between the start and the end of any journey, the distance between your reality and your dream, is a difficult place to navigate. But we are not alone. The first part of Hebrews 12:1 tells us there is a cloud of witnesses cheering us on. Giants of faith who celebrate every step we take. Hidden in this cloud is a man named Noah. Just a regular guy who built an ark as the sun split the trees. His cheers to you today: 'Keep going. Obey God, even when it doesn't make sense. One day, you will see God's promise. So, tighten up those laces. Stay in your track. And keep running.'

Amongst the cheers, there are shouts from a woman named Sarah. A woman who miraculously conceived a child way beyond childbearing years. Her chants to you today: 'Keep going. God is faithful to His word. If He said it, He will do it. So, tighten up those laces. Stay in your track. And keep running.'

And don't forget about Moses. A man who led an entire nation out of captivity. One who saw God's goodness in little flakes of manna and God's greatness in His ability to split seas. He bellows: 'Keep going. The finish line is near. No matter what obstacles you face, God will see you through. So, tighten up those laces. Stay in your track. And keep running.'

One by one, cheer after cheer, a mighty symphony of shouts resound for you and me. Yes, we have a cloud. God's chosen cheerleaders. But we also have a crowd. Cheerleaders of our own choosing. People we spend time with. People we listen to. People whose words we give weight to. Friend, if their cheers lead you, be sure they lead you well. Their cheers will either release you or restrict you. Their words will either build you up or bring you down. Their opinions will either spur you on or rule you out. If people in your world are advising you to lower your standards to get a date, you will chase their cheers to places you don't want to go. If people in your world are telling you to stop waiting for God's best and settle for what is on offer right now, you will chase their cheers to places you never wanted to visit.

A good cheerleader will encourage you to push through your struggle, to keep going when you want to give up. A good cheerleader has the faith to see your soon-to-be success, even when you don't have enough energy to lift your own head. Surround yourself with good people. Godly people. People who will cheer for you in the messy, middle moments of life.

Many times over the past few years I have asked God why I am single. Today, I look around and see why.

When you consider your life right now, there will be some people ahead of you. For me, this is Sara. A godly, married woman who unknowingly encouraged me to write this book. Sara is an already published author. Someone further along the track than I am. But Sara spoke purpose into my single season and gave me the courage to write these words to you. We all need people ahead of us. People to encourage us. Help us. Advise us. Challenge us. Teach us. Her success does not hinder me, it helps me.

There will be others running right alongside you. For me, this is Vic. Remember our awkward encounter a few years ago at the church event? For many years, we sat side by side on the single tram. We cried together. We laughed together. We prayed together. We learnt together. God knew we needed each other, and we certainly did. But let me give you a little update. Remember our hashtag for the year 2020, the year of miracles? For Vic, this involved her exiting the single tram and finding herself a six-foot-something male and a sparkly, diamond ring. For me, I finished this book. Her race is not mine. I'm learning that. Maybe we both got our miracles after all.

And there will be others coming up behind you. For me, this is Rebecca. I recently attended another wedding. Thankfully, I was nearing the end of my book-writing journey and had learnt a few things to help me cope better on days like this. But I will never forget how easy the sound of wedding bells could crush a single heart. I could see what her smiles were hiding. We differed in age but our questions were the same. *Is this ever going to be me?* In that moment, my breakups were her breakups. My problems were her problems. My issues were her issues. My fears were her fears. My insecurities were her insecurities. I could hold her hand because I, too, had walked this path. I could comfort her with more than just words, but with life-changing truth dripped in real-life experience. Truth that had freed my heart, and my hands, to take hold of God's good promises for me. Truth that could free her heart, and her hands, too.

This is how God works. He beautifully weaves the lives of many while focusing on the precious life of one. Remember the empty bedroom in my house? This room was home to a young woman in serious need of a place to stay. My empty dining room table created a safe place for a friend whose marriage was in turmoil. The empty space in my diary allowed me to dedicate many days to write these words to you. You see, His pace for your journey not only protects and positions you. It also protects and positions others too. Pauses in your journey are not postponements. Pauses are intentionally woven into your journey for your good. Her good too. Delays in your journey are not denials. Delays are intentionally woven into your journey for your good. Her good too. Slow-moving seasons are not to prevent you from reaching your goal. Slow-moving seasons are to ensure that you do, and you accompany others as you go.

I still hate running. Fact. I don't think this will ever change. But I am changing.

And maybe that's the point?

CHAPTER 7

It's (Maybe Not That) Complicated

OK, so let's recap. The enemy knows he can alter our race if he can alter our pace. He wants to stop us from reaching God's beautiful plans for our lives. And one sure way to stop me in my tracks today, is to give me a decision.

Decisions and me are not a good mix. If we were to go on holiday, I'd let you decide the place and time. Sure, you know me. I'll go anywhere, anytime. And if we were to watch a movie, I'd allow you to pick which one. Action. Rom-com. Thriller. I honestly don't mind. You choose.

Maybe I'm being flexible. Maybe I'm easy-going. Maybe I just want you to be happy. Or maybe, just maybe, I don't like making decisions. Yes, I'm the kind of girl who downloads the menu days before a new restaurant visit. I've learnt it saves time. Precious food-eating time. And with every minute that passes with the server hovering over me, I only get more and more confused and less and less decisive.

There are just too many options. Often, too many good options. So, I have learnt to make my choice in advance. I'll still ask the server to rhyme off the specials. You know, got to make it look believable. I'll hmm and I'll ponder. I'll pause and I'll wonder. They don't know I made up my mind days before I ever sat in that booth. And with one final scan over the menu, my lips moving as I pretend to read, I will deliver my rehearsed order with unassuming confidence. *I'll have the chicken strips drizzled in sweet chilli sauce with a side of garlic fries. Make that a large Diet Coke. Oh, and can I have a straw? Please and thank you.*

When it comes down to it, I guess I just don't want to make the wrong decision. Nobody ever does, do they? I mean, is there anything worse than making a spontaneous food order, only later to regret it? So instead I plan. And I plan in advance. No panic-ordering. No last minute changes. Stick to what I know and prepare as best I can for the unexpected. That means, having a back-up order ready to go, if for some reason they no longer serve chicken strips.

Yes, I like to plan.

But I can't plan for everything.

A friend tells me she has been to this restaurant before and the lasagne is incredible. *Yum. I do like lasagne. Maybe I should give that a go instead?* Everybody else decides to order a starter. *I suppose I should too. Well, that changes everything. I can't get chicken for starter and main, can I?* The menu has been updated and the restaurant no longer serves chicken strips. And they just ran out of lasagne, my recently changed back-up order. *Seriously, what am I meant to choose now?*

Options. Options. Options.

Decisions. Decisions. Decisions.

For me, too many options equal too many opportunities to pick the wrong one and too many unforeseen obstacles to always confidently pick the right one. Options get me flustered and all kinds of confused. And before I know it, I'm left chewing over my own bad choice and washing it down with a tall glass of regret. It's just so very complicated, isn't it?

Life is full of decisions. Thousands upon thousands of decisions every single day. One decision after the other. Each one somehow leading onto the next. Some big. Some small. Some expected. Some unexpected. And for a girl who likes to download menus, life can be seriously overwhelming and somewhat exhausting.

Recently I found myself paralysed by the pressure of decision-making once again. Following the disappointment of a job interview fail, I found myself wandering the streets of uncertainty. It would seem I'm as good at interviews as I am at decision-making. Anyway. Abruptly faced with an unexpected stop and forced to give way to someone else, I was caught at a crossroad of life. Faith reminded me that God can use closed doors to redirect to open doors elsewhere. So, I wondered if maybe, just maybe, God was calling me into something different. Something new. But fear restricted me. Imagine the world's largest menu with every single job to ever exist splayed across its pages. I was holding it. I was studying it. The pressure to make a decision was mounting and I was panicking. Should I pursue this path or that path? Should I turn left or right? Should I stay here or go there?

Options. Options. Options.

Decisions. Decisions. Decisions.

This is the pattern of my life. I consider all the options. I weigh up the good and bad of each one. I make lists. I make lists of lists. I pray, and pray some more. I even consult my Bible and look to it as my guide. And yet, somehow, I get stuck. Paralysed by fear of getting it so wrong. Debilitated by worry of somehow missing what is right. Unable to move forward. Unable to turn back. Unable to decide. Just stuck.

It should come as no surprise to you that this pattern follows me in my pursuit of my perfect love story too. I think it follows many of us single girls. Watch how this pattern unfolds in my life.

Should I apply for this job? Because maybe, just maybe, Mr Right will work in the office beside mine. One day, we will bump into one another at the photocopier. Casual conversations about the weekend tells me he goes to church. The Scripture tattoo along his arm and old-school WWJD bracelet confirms my sneaky suspicion. *Wait, you're a Christian too?* Boom. Happily ever after.

The End.

Should I move to America? Because maybe, just maybe, that's where my future husband lives. I will move into his sister's neighbourhood. She thinks we will be a great match. And do you know what – she's right. He's been praying for me, his Belfast girl. And I've been waiting for him, my American boy. Boom. Happily ever after. The End.

At one point, I was so worried I would miss the small window of opportunity to meet my other half, I even overthought a trip to Starbucks. Not. Even. Kidding. But what if I missed the chance for him to write my name and his number on my oversized coffee cup? And that's before I even try to figure out if *Mr Right Now* is *Mr Right For Me* by the time I finish the contents of said coffee cup. Oh, I despair. How overwhelming. How exhausting. And yet, so very me.

When finding love and getting married is something we so desperately hope awaits in our future, we can feel the heavy weight of every single decision we face today. Today's decisions are difficult to make when feeling overwhelmed by tomorrow's dream.

But remember: faith walks, fear stops. Fear paralyses us, immobilises us and entangles us. Fear debilitates us and disables us. It weighs us down with worry and prevents us from making progress by feeding into continuous cycles of doubt. Fear stops, and isn't this exactly what the enemy wants?

Many times I have allowed the paralysing effects of fear to grip my life. I feel tossed back and forth by waves of uncertainty. Driven by currents into uncharted territory. Battered by all kinds of unpredictability and washed up upon the shores of unrest and uneasiness. I freeze. Not because I want to, but because I feel powerless not to. The fear of missing out and the fear of messing up is enough to stop any girl in her tracks. We want to make the right decision. The perfect decision. And making the perfect decision just seems downright impossible to me.

And that's because it is. Many of us accept that perfection does not exist. We watch it play out on movie screens. We notice it unfold in the lives of others on social media. But deep down, many of us know that frozen food aisles do not always lead to love and social media posts are often highlight reels, not bloopers of real life. Yes, we can accept that perfection does not exist. And yet, we still somehow expect perfection to feature in our life stories. Ah yes, the perfect decision leading to the perfect partner leading to the perfect marriage. Which right now, equals perfect chaos as I face every single decision with the analytical precision required to get me there.

Sometimes we would rather stop, than step wrong. This is the paralysis of perfection. Sometimes we would rather miss one step, than misstep. This is the paralysis of perfection. Sometimes we would rather freeze, than fail. This is the paralysis of perfection. And this is one sure way of stopping any girl on her God-assigned journey.

In 1 Peter 5:8 we are warned, 'the devil prowls around like a roaring lion looking for someone to devour'. But check out the context of this warning given in the verses just before;

'Humble yourselves, therefore, under God's mighty hand, that he may lift you up in due time. *Cast all your anxiety on him because he cares for you.*'

1 PETER 5:6–7, emphasis mine

You see, the enemy prowls around those weighed down with worry. The enemy growls around those cast down with care. The word for anxieties used here comes from the Greek word *merizō*, which means 'to separate or divide a person into various parts'. And doesn't that perfectly describe how we feel when faced with decisions sometimes? We follow every possible decision to every possible outcome. We feel the divide and simply cannot decide.

A roaring lion is not a predator who is trying to sneak up or pounce on its victim unexpectedly. No, a lion roars to intimidate his prey. Because sometimes, he doesn't have to do much else. Sometimes our enemy takes a back seat, only to watch us drown in the depths of own decision-making, overwhelm us in the ocean of options and mesmerise us in the sea of multiple choice. He circles around us, as we circle around decisions. Over and over and over again. Moving from one option to the next, yet never moving forwards. The paralysis of perfection. Over the years, I have often viewed fear as a friend. Something to protect me from making an imperfect decision and prevent me from landing in a complete mess. But imperfect people living in an imperfect world simply cannot make perfect decisions. We can however make good decisions. We can make wise decisions. We can make God-honouring decisions. Friend, fear does not come from God (2 Tim. 1:7). Fear is not a friend that protects or prevents us from making imperfect decisions. Fear is a foe that simply prohibits us from making any decision at all.

Let's lay the illusion of perfection down and begin to ask the right question: How do we make good decisions today as we continue to navigate this single season?

God stepped into the chaos of my choices on a sunny Saturday afternoon. This Saturday was like many others gone before. Steady pace. Regular rhythm. And I got to hang out with Marcus. Let me describe him for you. Marcus is unlike any other person you will ever meet. Fact. Entering this world weighing no more than a small bag of sugar, his first year of life was spent merely fighting to survive. Born at only 24 weeks, the odds of survival were stacked high against him. The doctors were uncertain of his future. His parents were too. Yet despite knocking on heaven's door a number of times, Marcus defied all odds and now stands, nearly taller than me, at the age of 16. I have watched Marcus grow from a little boy in nursery, unable to walk and unable to talk, into an incredible young man. One who now runs circles around me and would talk to a brick wall if he thought it would answer. Also a fact.

Lots of things about Marcus have changed over the years, but one thing definitely has not: his fighting spirit. Despite countless surgeries and procedures, endless setbacks and challenges, this kid always seems to come back stronger. There is much to learn from a person like Marcus. And this day was no different.

It was our ten-year 'carer-versary'. An anniversary for carers. A 'carer-versary'. Trust me, when relationship anniversaries aren't on the cards, this is certainly an occasion to celebrate. To mark this special day, I decided to take Marcus to a popular high ropes course in Belfast. Nothing quite says, 'Thank you for being awesome over the past ten years' than suspending someone over thirty feet in the air, right?

His eyes widened with excitement when I first told him of my plans. This was new. This was fun. This was a day for adventure. We stood side by side; feet firmly planted on the ground and gazed up to the sea of obstacles that hovered over our heads. One obstacle after the other, each one leading onto the next. Unstable wooden bridges. Rickety horizontal ladders. Single rope balance beams. Each obstacle different from the last. Each one varying in difficulty. We silently watched as others manoeuvred their way around the course above our heads. Each person taking one step, facing one obstacle, making one decision, at a time. Their own pace. Their own journey. Their own adventure.

What a picture of life. Each day filled with decisions to make and opportunities to take, obstacles to face and challenges to embrace. Just a group of people, journeying side by side. Each person on their own unique journey. Each person embracing their own kind of adventure.

I glanced at Marcus. His eyes now a mixture of excitement and nervousness. His smile had subtly lowered as he began to analyse the course above. *Where am I meant to start? Where is the end? How do I get over that? Around that? Under that? Through that? What happens if I stumble and my foot somehow slips? What if I take a wrong turn? What if I get stuck in the middle? Who is going to help me then?*

Each question, never spoken but written all over his face. Despite any reservations, Marcus stepped each leg into the harness and began his ascent. Cautious yet persistent. Slow yet steady. The attendant attached his harness to the immovable metal frame above his head and he was ready to go. His adventure could begin.

I stood below Marcus that day and I tracked his movements and followed his steps. I was his own personal cheerleader. His very own private coach. I shouted pieces of encouragement and I bellowed my advice to help him on his way. And this was the moment. The moment I heard the voice of God. Now, it wasn't audible. I haven't experienced that. Well, not yet anyway. But it was clear. So very clear. God has a beautiful way of speaking extraordinary things in ordinary moments of life. And He certainly did that day. In the middle of a packed adventure park, God stood right beside me and He told me to listen to the words of advice and encouragement I was giving to Marcus. These were God's words to me and my decision-divided heart. And if you have ever felt the paralysis of perfection and struggled to make a decision too, maybe these are His words to you too.

'Start with a little step and take it one step at a time'
The choice was his. Turn right or go left. Challenge one or challenge two. Route one or route two. Marcus stood at the start of the course with options.

Ugh. Options. My favourite.

I often think how life would be much easier if God would just tell us audibly what to do. No place for mistakes. No wiggle room for error. Maybe if He used some sort of megaphone, one big enough to be heard from the throne room of heaven. Loud and clear. Or maybe He could paint the sky with a roadmap to our lives or arrange the clouds to spell out His plans. Nice and simple. And yet, He chooses not to. Instead, God invites us into the conversation. God is not some militant God, one who places inflexible itineraries, stringent schedules and rigid details on every aspect of our lives. No, Father God warmly invites each of us to navigate life's journey with Him. Believing God has strict plans only serves to restrict us. Believing He has binding conditions will only leave us bound by fear, thinking we might miss something out or mess something up.

Let me remind you of one of the most quoted verses in the Bible:

> 'Trust in the Lord with all your heart, and do not lean on your own understanding. In all your ways acknowledge him, and he shall make straight your paths.'
> **PROVERBS 3:5–6, ESV**

'Acknowledge' is a funny word. I can acknowledge cake is bad for me, but choose to eat the whole thing anyway. I can acknowledge my house needs cleaning, but choose to ignore that too. This kind of acknowledgement does not require action. But the Hebrew word for 'acknowledge' is *yada* which means 'to know'. 'In all your ways *know* God and he will make your paths straight.' This kind of acknowledgement certainly requires action.

Remember, a woman who knows God, will know His ways. A woman who knows God, will know His will. The will of God is not some puzzle for us to piece together or some sort of riddle for us to solve. When you read God's Word, it is obvious that some decisions of life are black and white. Right and wrong. Sometimes what God wants you to do is as clear as that. But I find it is not the black and white decisions of life that often stop us girls in our tracks. I mean, many of us do not lie awake at night deliberating whether to kill someone or not. In case you aren't sure, that is black and white. Don't do it. End of. No, it is often those little grey decisions of life that keep us tossing and turning. If only there was a specific instruction contained within the New Testament letters which would help me discern if I should try online dating one more time. Or if only there was some law hidden in the book of Leviticus which would help me decide whether I should accept his offer of a second date or not. Or whether I should change job. Or move to America. Or visit Starbucks. But aren't these the kind of decisions that stop us in our tracks? The kind of decisions that are less black and white and a lot more grey.

But what if they are intentionally painted grey by God? What if some decisions of life are meant to be less black and white and more grey because God actually wants us to choose? Friend, you will know the right step to take, when in step with the heartbeat of God. Imitation follows intimacy. We talked about this in Chapter Five, but I think it's worth saying again. Us single Jesus girls get so caught up trying to figure out the perfect will of God, that we get caught out by fear of somehow missing it or messing with it. Knowing what step to take next comes from a place of knowing God intimately now. You must know Him well, to follow Him well. That means, when you decide to spend time reading His Word, your decisions will better align with His. Knowing Him is found in the black and white print contained on those very pages. That means, when you decide to spend time in prayer, your decisions will better align with His. Knowing Him is found by listening to His voice. That means, when you decide to worship instead of worry, your decisions will better align with His. Knowing Him is found by simply being in His presence. That means, when you decide to enjoy community with His Church, your decisions will better align with His. Knowing Him is found by rubbing shoulders with His children. When you know Him well, you can follow Him well. And doesn't He promise to lead us somewhere unimaginably good?

Good decisions allow God to lead the way. But how often do we make decisions based on our own feelings or emotions? Loneliness. Sadness. Insecurity. Anger. Jealousy. Bitterness. All very real emotions. All very real emotions I have experienced too. But if allowed, emotions will lead us to places we never want to go, and keep us there longer than we ever thought we would stay. For example, if we feel lonely and then make a decision to date someone from this place of loneliness, who knows where we might end up. Restless hearts can often make reckless decisions. Or if we feel insecure and then make a decision to text that person we already know is not right for us, who knows where this might lead us. There is no judgment here. I wear the badge of bad decisions too. But instead of allowing our feelings to lead our decision-making, what if we allow our feelings to lead us to God? In doing so, we allow Him to deal with our feelings first, so we can better follow His leading instead.

After some time deliberating, Marcus selected his route. He chose left. And he cautiously placed one foot on the rope to begin his journey. He completed obstacle one and then faced his next decision. Route one or route two. Left or right. This time, Marcus chose right. Again, he placed one foot on the rope and continued his journey. This is when I noticed something beautiful. Neither option was wrong. Marcus was never going to take a wrong turn. The course was already outlined. The path was already set. Of course, some routes took longer than others. Some routes were harder and much more challenging to navigate. Some obstacles may have been avoidable and some challenges may have been escapable. But the course was already mapped out. Mapped out by someone else. He just had to walk in it.

In Psalm 37, after King David talks about bending our desires to align with God's desires, he continues with this:

> 'The Lord makes firm the steps of the one
> who delights in him'
> **PSALM 37:23**

What an encouragement. God makes firm our steps. They are ordered and ordained, appointed and approved. The course of your life has already been mapped out. Singled out. Sometimes it's not about getting from A to B to C in a perfectly planned and sequential order. Sometimes it's not about turning right or going left. It's about completing the course as best you can, with God as your personal cheerleader and private coach guiding you along the way (Psa. 32:8). Sometimes both options will look equally good. Sometimes both right *and* left will honour God. Sometimes both route one *and* route two will please God. God has given us the ability to discern what is best (Phil. 1:9). He simply invites us to choose and promises to go with us (Isa. 30:21). We just need to take one day at a time. One step at a time. One God-honouring decision at a time.

When I think about it, I'm pretty glad God doesn't own a

megaphone. Or chooses not to use it with me anyway. How many of us would be where we are today if God told us years in advance that this is what today would look like? Maybe we would have got ahead of ourselves. Got started before we were ready. Or maybe we would have given up before we even took the first step. I certainly would have.

Let me tell you how my book-writing journey started for me. Many years ago, a friend asked me to write something for an organisation in our church. Something small. No big deal. He needed my help, so I said yes. This girl with no writing experience whatsoever said yes. *What was I thinking?* But little did I know this was the small beginning of something much bigger than I ever could have thought or imagined. Soon after the breakup, I felt the gentle nudge of God to start an Instagram page. A place to share my love for God and newfound love for writing. Something small. No big deal. So again, I said yes. *I mean, what's the harm in a little ol' Instagram page, right?* Another year later, the gentle nudge of God prodded my heart once more. This time with something a little bigger. Maybe God wanted me to write a devotional, or possibly write a book one day. The details were fuzzy. The logistics were vague. The specifics were unknown and the instructions felt incomplete. But with a quick intake of breath and a little stretch of faith, again I said yes. And the gentle nudge of God guided me to a shop the next day to purchase a secondhand laptop. Over the next few months, I started to write. About God. Life. Stuff. Then came the gentle nudge.

Seriously, God – a book about being single?! Not quite a nudge this time. Something a lot less gentle and a lot more uncomfortable. I didn't particularly want my personal life, my struggles, my worries, my fears, printed in black and white for anyone and everyone to see. But a simple conversation with an old friend over coffee made me realise that this next step was the right step. So, with a deep intake of breath and every ounce of faith I could muster, I said yes. Let me tell you, the girl who said yes to writing that small piece for church that day, would not have said yes to writing a book about being single. That girl would have laughed. Seriously laughed. The nervous kind of laughter. The kind you do when in utter disbelief and feeling all kinds of awkward. And then, with all the reverence in the world, she would have politely declined the offer and suggested something else. Anything else. You see, we can easily reject our future if we project too far into the future. But big decisions don't seem so big when we allow God to partner with us in the small decisions that lead us there. Sometimes, it is the seemingly insignificant steps we take in the seemingly insignificant moments of life that will have the most significance in our journeys. And sometimes, God will use even our smallest 'yes' to invite us on our biggest adventure yet.

Friend, God will tell you everything you need to know to make every decision you need to make today. Next moves are not often given over megaphones, they are revealed in simple conversations over coffee with a godly friend. Or shared quietly with you in the middle of a busy adventure park on a typical Saturday afternoon. Next steps are not often revealed by glaringly obvious neon signs or meticulously placed cloud designs. No, next steps are often highlighted in your Bible or echoed in the sweet whispers of worship. In His wisdom, God doesn't release the whole story. He doesn't reveal the whole path. But He will show you the next step. In Psalm 119:105, we are told 'Your word is a lamp for my feet, a light on my path'. In those days, they didn't have spotlights to illuminate large areas. Instead, they used lamps. Just a small light to illuminate immediate surroundings. His Word is a lamp. Just enough light to allow us to see the next step. But not enough light for us to feel overwhelmed by the whole path. His Word will light the way, maybe just not the whole way. And boy, am I ever so glad.

'Don't worry, the harness will always catch you'

I don't know many people who wake up in the morning and say, 'Hey, what a great day to make a wrong decision.' Nobody wants to take a wrong turn. Nobody wants to get sidetracked by mistakes or sidestepped by mess-ups. Nobody wants to get backtracked by dead ends or detoured by failures.

But life happens and we are human. Imperfect humans who live in an imperfect world who cannot make perfect decisions.

If you have been 'adulting' for more than a day or two, you will know that you can plan your steps, you can prepare your route, but you cannot predict the future. With every decision we make in life, there always comes a degree of uncertainty. Ventures into unknown territory will always come with a level of unpredictability. Life doesn't exactly come in the form of a fully-exposed high ropes course. But that's when faith kicks in. You see, fear will prohibit you from making a decision, but faith will protect you. Because you know that even if you misstep or miss a step, God can always be trusted to bring something good out of it anyway. We will never be able to work everything out. We aren't God, but we can be godly and make God-honouring decisions. Sometimes we just need to allow God to be God and trust Him to work everything out for us. Our imperfections included.

Marcus' first step was a scary one. He gingerly stepped one foot onto the obstacle ahead of him. His hands whitened as he clung onto the rope above his head. His foot momentarily began to shake. Despite knowing he was secure, in that moment, he was unsure. He placed his foot back onto the platform and tugged firmly on the harness. I could see Marcus felt safe on the platform. It didn't jiggle up and down. It didn't sway back and forth with the wind of unpredictability. The platform was comfortable. Familiar. It felt secure. Safe. He could have opted to stay on the platform. He could have stayed where he was. Because fear craves familiarity. It keeps you static in places you know, for longer than you were ever meant to stay.

But his security never came from the platform. It came from the harness to which he was attached. Much like us. When you accept Jesus as your Saviour, you are automatically connected to an immovable source. He is our harness. Our anchor. Tested and trustworthy. Unshakeable and unchanging. Safe and secure.

King David continues in Psalm 37 with this:

> 'though he may stumble, he will not fall; for the
> LORD upholds him with his hand'
> **PSALM 37:24**

It's true – some life decisions may divert us and detour us. But this is the promise. You will never fall beyond His grip of grace.

Marcus knew he couldn't fall, yet his demeanour told a different story. Head knowledge doesn't always help when ropes are shaky and paths are tricky. Initially, Marcus had little need for the harness. He clung onto each rope as if his life depended on it. He conquered the first obstacle using upper body strength alone. His confidence grew. His feet gained momentum. Then out of absolutely nowhere, his foot slipped. Panic washed over his face and he was stunned to silence. For once. His face slowly regained colour and then he began to laugh. With relief, he proclaimed what I always knew to be true: 'Paula, you really can't fall!'

You see, it only took one misplaced step, one little slip, for Marcus to fully grasp that his safety, security and stability had nothing to do with him, and everything to do with what he was attached to. Friend, the success of your journey is not based on your navigational skills. It is not dependent on how skilfully you can master rope-walking or conquer every challenge you face. It is not reliant on whether you choose route A or route B, or whether you always get it right. Your safety, security and stability is always in the Person to whom you are attached. Always is. Always will be.

'And don't forget to have fun'
I watched Marcus extensively analyse every foot placement before he took every single step. He scrutinised every decision. He evaluated every move. Pure grit and resolve was written all over his face. He was going to finish this thing, one way or another. He was determined, yes. But was he having fun? No. This day for adventure had somehow morphed into just another challenge for him to overcome. Fear of failure will zap the fun right out of anything, won't it?

Boy, this one hit me hard. Without realising it, every dream I had for future days hung in the balance of me getting everything right every single time. Talk about insurmountable pressure. My face had developed wrinkles. My mind was in turmoil. My stomach was in knots and the joy-joy-joy-joy of the Lord was so far down I could hardly see it anymore.

Friend, in attempts to stifle God's promise of life to the full, the enemy will come to steal our joy, kill our laughter and destroy the very wonder of life itself (John 10:10). Please hear me. This is not some hall-pass to do what you want, when you want, with whom you want, wherever you want. Decisions will always have consequences. We will talk more about this is the next chapter. But this is meant to free you. Deciding to follow Jesus is the best decision you can, and will, ever make. Life with Him is an adventure to be enjoyed, not a military operation to endure. That's what makes our journey with God a relationship, not a dictatorship. It's meant to be you and Him in partnership. Father and daughter doing life together. The Christian life is meant to be an adventure and adventures require you to go for it. It's in the name after all. Adventures require you to add a little venture to your day. Take the plunge and dive into certain unknowns. Take the risk and go for it. Turn right or go left. Either way, invite God on your adventure and smile as you go. Why not order something spontaneous off the menu for a change and have a little fun.

Take one step at a time. Make one God-honouring decision at a time. And enjoy the journey as you go. Just you and Him. Maybe it doesn't have to be so complicated after all.

CHAPTER 8

No Strings Attached

Confession time. Sometimes options are not the problem. I know what God wants me to do today. Sometimes obedience is the problem. Because I don't always like what God wants me to do today.

When I first felt the not-so-gentle nudge of God to write this book, it didn't stop me asking for this single season to end. Believe me. I so desperately wanted the end of my story, this story, to read 'happily ever after'. My version. Deep down I knew God wanted me to write this book. This was a step of obedience. A step forwards in faith I was willing to take. But deep, deep down, I knew God wanted me to write this book single. This was another step of obedience. One, I thought, which took me further away from my dream, not closer to it. A step backwards I was not so willing to take. So, I begged as I wrote. I cried as I learnt.

I pleaded as I prayed. Only for my persistent requests to bounce off my bedroom wall and return to sender with a label which simply read this: 'No.'

Such a small word, isn't it?

A small word often followed by a big hurt.

Many of us accept that God *can* say 'no'. He is God after all and He has the power and authority to do so. But the idea that God *does* say 'no', particularly when this is His response to something good and something we really want, and really want now; this is a lot harder to wrap our heads and our hearts around, right? As you read these words today, my guess is you are still single. If not and you have recently made a new love connection, I am so happy for you. Your race is not mine. But most of us, we still ride the single tram. And any desire or request for a relationship right now has been met with that same dreaded reply.

'No.'

As we continue this journey together, it's time we address one of the biggest fears that can stop single Jesus girls in their journey today. And that is, what if His 'no' today, is actually 'no, not ever'? What if I have this 'gift of singleness' people talk about? Sadly, I have watched many girls allow the disappointment of singleness to stop them walking with God altogether. The world can offer options that look so appealing to a hurting heart. And sometimes chasing your dream with the fast pace of society seems much better than pacing your journey with the steady, sometimes slower, heartbeat of God. Friend, this is a difficult chapter for me to write. An even more difficult one to learn. But if we want God's very best plans to unfold in our lives, it's important that we do. So let's tackle this one together. But first, let's reset. Remember, we aren't designed to live in the future. We are designed to thrive right now. The enemy will only use the 'what ifs' of tomorrow and the 'noes' of not yet, to stop us in our tracks. So let's fix our focus again on today and figure out how we might learn to accept His 'no' for right now?

In Matthew 7, Jesus teaches us something about this. He begins:

> 'Ask and it will be given to you; seek and you will find; knock and it will be opened to you. For everyone who asks receives; the one who seeks finds; and to the one who knocks, the door will be opened.'
>
> **MATTHEW 7:7–8**

Sounds amazing and so very simple, right? Just ask, and you will receive. Just seek, and you will find. Just knock, and the door will open. No empty hands. No lost causes. No closed doors. And certainly, no noes. And yet, the reality of today will tell us that when we ask for a husband, he doesn't just suddenly appear on our doorstep. Instead, we only seem to lose heart when we seek to find love and get knocked back further with disappointment after disappointment. Day after day. No after no. Suddenly a big question mark hovers over this promise for us single girls. We ask, but we aren't getting. We seek, but we aren't finding. And we knock, knock, knock, only to discover no man is ever on the other side of any door. Fear floods in. Faith rushes out. And feet want to stop.

But Jesus doesn't end there, and neither should we. That's only half the promise. That's only half the truth. And might I suggest this is exactly what the enemy wants you to read. You see, half-truths are his speciality. His tactical game plan ever since the beginning. Let's trace this tactic all the way back to the Garden of Eden and for a moment, imagine the opening scenes of creation. God's words wrapped form around every particle and substance. Every living and non-living creature. Both day and night. Land and sea. Man and woman. Each one beautifully designed and uniquely created and intricately crafted. Beauty flowed through every river and goodness graced every flower. And everything was good. Perfection was the anthem of Eden. No sickness. No sadness. No sin. And mankind was free.

- Free to have *relationship*

'So God created mankind in his own image, in the image of God he created them; male and female he created them.' (Gen. 1:27)

'The LORD God said, "It is not good for the man to be alone. I will make a helper suitable for him."...

'So the LORD God caused the man to fall into a deep sleep; and while he was sleeping, he took one of the man's ribs and then closed up the place with flesh. Then the LORD God made a woman from the rib he had taken out of the man, and he brought her to the man.' (Gen. 2:18, 21–22)

- Free to *rule*

God blessed them and said to them, "Be fruitful and increase in number; fill the earth and subdue it. Rule over the fish in the sea and the birds in the sky and over every living creature that moves on the ground."' (Gen. 1:28)

'The LORD God took the man and put him in the Garden of Eden to work it and take care of it.' (Gen. 2:15)

- Free to *choose*

'Now the LORD God had formed out of the ground all the wild animals and all the birds in the sky. He brought them to the man to see what he would name them; and whatever the man called each living creature, that was its name. So the man gave names to all the livestock, the birds in the sky and all the wild animals. But for Adam no suitable helper was found.' (Gen. 2:19–20)

And the LORD God commanded the man, "You are free to eat from any tree in the garden; but you must not eat from the tree of the knowledge of good and evil, for when you eat from it you will certainly die."' (Gen. 2:16–17)

Yes, Adam and Eve were gifted with free choice. Just like us. They could eat whatever they liked, from wherever they liked, with only one restriction. To not eat from the tree of knowledge of good and evil. And there we have it: God's first 'no'. This word isn't new to God's vocabulary. And although it might feel like it sometimes, it isn't only reserved for us and our love lives either. God can say 'no'. God does say 'no'. And it is in this context that the enemy makes his first appearance and spits his script of lies: 'Did God really say, "You must not eat from *any* tree in the garden?"' (Gen. 3:1, emphasis mine).

Notice how Satan misquoted God's words. He repeated most. He omitted some. He altered others. God didn't say they mustn't eat from *any* tree. He did say they mustn't eat from *one* tree. How subtle. How clever. How convincing. And how very dangerous. Close enough to the truth to sound believable. Far enough away from the truth to cause utter devastation. Satan wanted Eve to believe she wouldn't die if she ate from the tree (Gen. 3:4). Satan wanted Eve to believe God was withholding something good from her when He said 'no' (Gen. 3:5). Satan wanted Eve to believe she knew better than God. Oh, how he can twist truth and misquote God's message so easily. He can, and he still does.

I see this very same pattern in my own life sometimes. I imagine Satan sliding in and luring me away with lies. 'Didn't God say He would give you everything you asked for? Why would God not give you what you want then? Maybe He isn't so good after all. Look at all the good things you are missing out on. Look at what God is giving to her. Look at what God is keeping from you. He is denying you so much. Stop following God's rules. Go after what you want.'

You see, the enemy roars to intimidate us, but he lies to confuse us. Half truths are simply full lies cleverly disguised. Friend, there are many lies the enemy will spout to try to trick us today. So, in love, I want to expose some of these lies to you. This is not to scare you or discourage you, but to teach you. Us girls need to detect the difference between words that tickle our ears to rest our hearts, and words that penetrate our ears to test our hearts. I don't need words that just sound good. Neither do you. We need words that are good. We need truth. The whole truth. And although a cleverly worded lie may hold elements of truth within it, half truths are full lies often dressed in their Sunday best. We must be careful when sweet-sounding statements and half truths land on our ears and clog up our newsfeed. Many sound biblical. Many sound right. Many sound incredibly good. But just like a tasty treat on a mousetrap, we can be easily enticed with what appears good, only to get stuck in dangers we never realised were there.

If we learn to detect his lies better, we can learn to reject his lies better. Better lie-detectors are better lie-rejecters. Sounds like some cheesy line from a terrible detective television series, but it's catchy. And I'd rather catch this phrase than get caught out by one of his lies. I'm guessing you would too.

So, back to Jesus' teaching in Matthew 7. Let's read those verses again, this time in the context of the full conversation. We don't want half the truth. We want the whole truth:

'Ask and it will be given to you; seek and you will find; knock and the door will be opened to you. For everyone who asks receives; and the one who seeks finds; and to the one who knocks, the door will be opened. Which one of you, if your son asks for bread, will give him a stone? Or if he asks for a fish, will give him a snake. If you, then, though you are evil, know how to give good gifts to your children, how much more will your Father in heaven give good gifts to those who ask him!'

MATTHEW 7:7–11

Now that changes things. Yes, God is the giver of good things, just not every thing we ask for. As I prepared to write this book, I followed many single Christian pages on social media. I wanted to know what messages were being communicated to people like you and me. I called it research. It sounded official. Anyway, there were little whispers of truth found in my endless scrolling. But these whispers were easily muted by a barrage of noise that bombarded my newsfeed and grabbed my attention. Once again, my single heart was captivated by blanket statements masquerading as beautiful Scripture and half truths posing as full facts. Well-intentioned writers encouraged readers to believe God's good plan surely meant a good man was on his way. And very, very soon. All we had to do was conceive it, believe it and receive it.

Conceive a good plan.

Believe this good plan matched God's good plan.

Receive this good plan.

I wrestled with my research. Truth is, God is God and He has the right to say 'no'. He cannot be manipulated into agreement with our plans. Remember, it is our desires that bend to align with His, not the other way around. He is the Parent. He is the Potter. He decides what to do with His children. He determines what He makes with His clay. But believing this alone means He becomes some domineering dictator that just says 'no' because He can. A half truth the enemy would be happy for you to accept. But God not only has the right to say 'no', He is right to say 'no' too.

When I was little, I thought having two older brothers was the best thing ever. My designated bodyguards. My private chauffeurs. My very own scapegoats who 'should have known better' when we all did something stupid. Amazing, until it's not. When I reached my early teens, I discovered the downside to being the baby in the family. Suddenly I was *too* young. I was *too* little. Too young to go there. Too little to do that. Too young to stay out to that time. My persistent requests were often met with a parental roadblock in the form of that dreaded two-letter word. No. Nothing I could say would change their minds. Parent's order trumped child's opinion, every single time.

As a young teenager, this seemed completely unfair. I wasn't asking for anything ridiculous. Or illegal. I just wanted a belly-button ring like her. Or to stay out past 11pm like them. Something simple. Something reasonable. Something good. And yet, 'no' was their resounding response. How unfair to a little girl who just wanted a belly-button ring and a later curfew. But how very kind to a 30-something-year-old woman who's thankful her belly-button remains ring-less and who understands the importance of sleep for a young mind and appreciates safety found at home late at night.

Only now do I understand that love is sometimes spelt with just two letters. You see, growing up my parents said 'no' to protect me. To teach me. To show me the right way. A better way. They knew me better than I knew myself. And they knew what was good for me. Not just for that moment, but for future moments too. Children don't always ask for good things. They ask for things that seem good one day, only to discover they are not so good the next. But good parents understand that a good gift today will still be good tomorrow.

This is the heart of Father God towards us too. Notice what Jesus does not say in Matthew 7:9–11. Nowhere does He say when a son asks his parent for bread, does he always get bread. Neither does He say when a son asks his parent for a fish, does he always get a fish. In fact, Jesus never tells us what the parent *gives*. Instead, Jesus tells us what the parent *withholds*. Here's what I think Jesus is saying here: good gifts are not confined to what is given alone, but are also defined by what is not given too.

Yes, the best kind of gift we can ever receive today is the kind of gift we really need. I've had many conversations with God about how marriage is good and so it just makes sense I should be married. And very, very soon. My argument is simple: if marriage is good and Your plans are good, then marriage must also equal Your plans. But the trouble is, I've missed out one key part of the equation. Marriage is good, yes. His plans are good, definitely. But is marriage actually His good plan *for me*? Is marriage actually His good plan for me *right now*? Oh, how I hope marriage is written into God's perfect plan for my life. I really do. But, right now, I have an assurance that each day He says 'no', it's for good reason. This is your assurance today too.

Our heavenly Father knows how to give good gifts to us. Sometimes these gifts come packaged in a cute little box. They are decorated in pretty wrapping paper, tied with a beautiful ribbon and given a tag that simply reads 'yes'. I like this kind of gift. I'm sure you do too. But sometimes His best gifts come packaged in something far more difficult to hold and much harder to open. These gifts don't come in pretty wrapping paper. They aren't tied with a beautiful ribbon. They simply come with that two-letter word scribed into its tag. I don't like these gifts as much. I don't think anyone does. But sometimes this is the kindest gift He could ever give us, because it's the kind of gift we so desperately need. There is so much goodness to be uncovered in gifts like this. When He says 'no' to something we think we want today because He actually knows what we need today. When He doesn't give us poor replicas of bread that would never fulfil us or dangerous substitutes for fish that have potential to harm us. Sometimes His loveliest gifts are in the form of 'no, not right' and instead 'not right, but try left'. He knows the difference between what we think is good and what He knows is unimaginably better. Between what we want right now and what He knows isn't right for now. Don't let disappointment make you see just one side of the story. Don't miss the goodness in a gift by reading only half of His message. Don't just accept half the truth. Unpack the whole truth. And remember to turn the tag over. You'll find it reads this: 'Love from your Father.' Every gift He gives is good, but these gifts will take different forms. His 'yes' and His 'no'. The give and the take. The open doors and closed doors. The rejection letters and sharp left turns. We won't always understand it. We won't always agree with it. We won't always like it. But when we trust the Gift-giver, we trust His gift is good too. The beautiful thing about God is, His authority and power to say 'no' always comes hand in hand with a deep, Fatherly love that always acts in our best interests. Unmet expectations do not equal unanswered prayers. It just means, our prayers are being answered differently, and even better than expected.

If it's for you, it might pass by you
There is a statement people throw about these days like confetti. It has certainly been flung in my direction a time or

two. It goes like this: 'If it's for you, it will not pass by you.' Oh, I like the sound of that. A promise to never miss out. That is good news. People toss these words towards my unmarried status to encourage me. They hurl it towards my hurting heart to comfort me. And sprinkle it over this season of singleness to reassure me. That yes, if God has planned it for me, it will surely happen to me.

I flicked through the pages of my Bible to find these sweet, sweet words. And I struggled. These words were not found among one of David's psalms. Or hidden in the wise sayings of Proverbs. Dear me. I could have sworn they were in there somewhere. But no. These words are not actually in the Bible at all. Go figure. I uncovered verse upon verse of how God does promise good plans for us. This we know is true. But nowhere does it say these good plans could never pass by us. In fact, the Bible is full of people who messed up, and then missed out, on certain things God planned for them. Ouch.

It's easy to mistake sweet-sounding statements for sweet promises in Scripture, isn't it? Well-intentioned people can unintentionally misinterpret God's Word sometimes. I certainly did. But like little shards of confetti, the words of this well-known phrase caught my heart off guard and left tiny cuts of confusion. *Is marriage actually God's plan for me? If so, does this mean I just do nothing until this unknown man picks me up as he passes by? Or maybe God's good plan for me doesn't involve marriage at all? What am I meant to do then?*

I contended with this confetti statement only to uncover another half truth many Christians believe today. But the full truth is this:

'If it's for you, it *might* pass by you.'

Friend, this is a sensitive topic. An unpopular one too. I get it. No part of me wants to believe I might never get married. Equally, no part of me wants to believe I can somehow miss God's good plan for my life. But as I opened God's Word, I received some clarity and instruction to help me on my journey today. I want to help you on yours too.

Again, the Garden of Eden sets the stage for the world's first example of 'if it's for you, it *might* pass by you'. Free choice welcomed sin into the world and God's perfect plan certainly passed by mankind. Perfection was no longer the anthem of Eden. Now sickness. Now sadness. Now sin. This was never God's intention, but a consequence of free choice. You see, freedom without choice is dictatorship. Freedom with choice is relationship. And relationship is the rhythm of God's heartbeat for humanity. Remember, God walked beside Adam and Eve in the Garden, not all over them. He desired authentic relationship with His creation and so He gifted mankind with the freedom to choose.

But freedom to choose is not freedom from *responsibility*. When you delve into Genesis, you see God gave Adam and Eve responsibility. To work the land. To keep the land. To subdue the land. To steward the land. To not eat from the tree of the knowledge of good and evil. With true freedom always comes responsibility.

Think about it like this; imagine we went to a buffet. Girl, you know I love my food. A portion of Chinese food, with a side of

Italian food, with a dollop of American food. All on one plate. What's not to love about that? Oh, and don't forget the side salad. You know, got to keep things balanced. At a buffet, everyone has freedom to choose what they want. Many options. Many combinations. Many, many plates. But some foods just don't sit well in an irritable tummy, do they? Some foods aren't so good for those with allergies. Or intolerances. Or slowing metabolisms. I mean, hello?! Yes, we have the freedom to choose, but we also have a responsibility to choose right. Food restrictions are not to prevent people from foods that are good. Food restrictions are to protect people from foods that are not good for them.

Food analogies always help me understand deep theology. And this one certainly helps me understand mankind's responsibility a little better. At a buffet, I am gifted free choice. I can make good choices. Or I can make bad choices and experience the consequences. A few extra pounds. A few sizes up. A few extra loo rolls. Likewise, we are gifted free choice each day we live on Earth. We can make good choices. Or we can make bad choices and experience the consequences. With true freedom always comes responsibility.

In Genesis, there was freedom to eat from any tree. Mankind could choose to obey and not eat from the tree of the knowledge of good and evil. Or mankind could choose to disobey and eat from the tree of the knowledge of good and evil. Mankind could choose to walk with God. Or mankind could choose to walk away from God. It was their choice then. And it's our choice now.

In today's society, many people want the power to choose without consequences. Many people want freedom to rule, but freedom from responsibility. These two things cannot be separated. They always come hand in hand. Sweet friend, God has good plans for your life. Unimaginably good plans. Better than you could ever want for yourself. I'm hoping if I write these words enough times they will cement in your heart and in mine. But God's sovereignty and our surrender always go together. You still have a part to play. I do too. So, do we choose to surrender our plans and our pace to align with His today, even if it's not what we want? Do we choose to submit our desires to His desires today, even if He says 'no' to our requests? The choice is ours.

Confession time again. Sometimes my big prayers for 'Thy will to be done' come with my terms and conditions subtly etched into the small print. Sometimes I want His will, I'm just unwilling to move His way. Sometimes I want a move of God, I just don't want to move where He is leading. It's true; a step of obedience may take you further away from your dream. For me, it was days spent delving into God's Word instead of days spent dating. It was nights spent at home alone with a secondhand laptop, instead of nights spent scrolling through dating apps. It was declining certain opportunities so that I might complete God's assignment. This assignment. This was my step of obedience. What's yours? I'm not talking about those grey decisions in life which God kindly invites you to choose with Him. I'm talking about those decisions in life that are black and white. The kind where God is not offering us options, but is simply asking us to obey. Maybe it's deleting dating apps you know are not good for you. Or to stop pursuing an unhealthy relationship you know isn't right. Or maybe it's to go on that mission trip overseas you have been delaying. Or to prioritise the project God has asked you to complete. A step of obedience will not always take you closer to your dream, but a step of obedience will always take you closer to His.

The Israelites knew something about this. Finally released from Egypt, they approached safety at last. Just another few steps and they would be completely safe and comfortably treading on the sandy shores of the desert. A place where Egyptian chariots would certainly sink and never dare to follow. The Israelites sat poised on the edge of the desert, ready to receive their next instruction. The sea on their right. The enemy behind. The promise straight ahead. I know what my next step would be. And turning back is most definitely not it. And yet, this is the very thing God commanded the Israelites to do (Exod. 14:1–2). Doesn't this seem like regression, not progression? The promise was ahead and God was asking them to step back. How confusing. But a step of obedience can often look like a step in the opposite direction to what makes sense. Obedience can seem to take you further away from the dream, not closer to it. But when we step in obedience, God steps in with the outcome.

You see, it was this very move of obedience that enticed Pharaoh and the Egyptians to pursue the Israelites. A move that would give God the glory and point many hearts towards Him. This one move perfectly positioned the Israelites for a sea-splitting miracle. A miracle they would have otherwise missed if they had not obeyed His command to turn back.

Friend, don't equate your progress in this journey with your position right now. Don't confuse forward steps with faith steps. Sometimes the biggest step of faith you can take today, is the step back of obedience He is asking you to make. Obedience is our key to unlocking God's good plan for our lives. The outcome is always His.

Not all orders will be easy to obey. There is a cost to following Jesus that many people would rather not acknowledge. Jesus Himself addressed this in Luke 9. Aware of His rapidly increasing popularity amidst a stream of incredible miracles and healings, Jesus placed high significance on telling prospective followers there was a cost to following Him. Jesus never promised following Him would be easy. Real life with Him is not miracle after miracle, healing after healing, 'yes' after 'yes'. To follow Jesus means we must give up certain things. Go without certain things. Surrender certain things. It's easy to follow Him when He gives us what we want, when we want it. It's easy to obey Him when we agree with what He has asked. It's easy to bend our plans to align with His when His plans align with ours. But too many people want to cross split seas, yet never carry their cross (Luke 9:23). We follow Jesus because of *who* He is, not because of *what* He does. So today, He invites us on an incredible adventure with Him. To choose when He offers. To obey when He doesn't. No strings attached.

As I have journeyed this single path with Jesus, there is another lesson I have had to learn. 'If-only' dreams can easily become 'only-if' obedience. Let me explain. One Sunday, on my way to church, I stopped at the cash machine to withdraw money to tithe. Like many Sundays, I typed in my PIN and I wondered if that empty seat beside me would ever be filled. I thought, 'If only God would answer my prayer.' I withdrew the cash and wondered if this little step of obedience would help me get one step closer to my dream. Week after week. Month and month. The same thought swirled around my mind as I stood at the cash machine. I was divided. Tithing is a step of obedience we are all asked to take. But I silently placed a caveat on my obedience and thought, 'God, if you bring me a husband, I will keep giving you my tithe.' I can be so rebellious sometimes. I wonder if you too have tried to bargain with God. We suggest that if God does something for us, we will do something for Him. Prayers like, 'God, *if only* you would do this, then I would do that.' slowly morph into 'God, *only if* you do this, will I do that'. Yes, an 'if-only' dream can easily become obedience. Sometimes we place caveats and conditions on our 'yes' to God. We attach strings to our steps in hopes we might persuade Him to give us what we want. Friend, your life offering is your option. But know this: what He asks us to do, He asks because He is good and He loves us. What He does, He does because He is good and He loves us. What He doesn't do, He doesn't do because He is good and He loves us. What He allows, He allows because He is good and He loves us. What He withholds, He withholds because He is good and He loves us. When He says 'yes', He says 'yes' because He is good and He loves us. When He says 'no', He says 'no' because He is good and He loves us. Allow these truths about God to dictate your circumstances. And then, allow these truths to dictate your response.

Holiness isn't the hottest topic in the global church today. But this is God's ultimate desire for every one of His children. To be holy. To be wholly His. Singleness is not a relationship status. Singleness is a heart status. An undivided heart with undivided devotion to God (Psa. 86:11). This is His desire for us regardless of our relationship status. That our hearts would not be distracted by the things of this world, but would remain singled out for His purpose, His plans and His promises. Do you know something – I don't think God is waiting for us to enthusiastically celebrate every closed door we face. I think He simply wants us to say 'OK' and follow Him anyway. Obedience is *our* responsibility. The outcome is *His*. Always.

Believe me, marriage is something I so want for my future, and I remain hopeful it might one day happen. This book writing process has not changed my desire to be a wife, but it is changing me. And maybe that's exactly why God is saying 'no' right now. Maybe this gift of singleness I have been given today isn't so bad after all. Sweet friend, we have this assurance: God is our good, good Father. One who only ever gives good gifts to His children. For some, this gift will be wrapped in a 'yes' and some tall, dark, handsome husband will come knocking on your door today. Or whatever your type may be. For others, this gift will be wrapped in a 'no' and come in the form of something a little different today. But always, a whole lot better. When we walk in His ways and say 'OK' to His orders, we walk straight into His very best plans for our lives (Deut. 6:18). And isn't this exactly what you want?

Me too, friend.

Me too.

CHAPTER 9

The Stretch of Progress

My heart was beating so hard, it was visibly bounding out of my chest. And my stomach was doing constant backflips. Like butterflies. Only these butterflies were at an unsupervised rave. My appetite had completely gone, which for a self-confessed foodie like me, is totally out of character. Eating is one of my all-time favourite hobbies. My hands were sweaty. My feet were unsteady. My focus was shaky. And my world felt as though it was spinning.

Now before you get too excited, this was not the start of my epic love adventure. This was not first date jitters or second date nerves. I hadn't caught the love bug or contracted the 'feels' for my supermarket guy. Unfortunately not. It took another unexpected trip to the Accident and Emergency department to confirm what was really going on. Please know, I rarely need medical assistance. It just so happens that when I do, they make for pretty good stories.

Vertigo.

I had vertigo.

Let me tell you; it could have been the opening scene to my beautiful love story because, of course, the most gorgeous doctor in the entire world was allocated my case. I can see the headline in lights: 'Dashing Doctor Meets Dizzy Damsel In Distress.' The story practically writes itself. Doctor McFittie signs off my prescription with his phone number. Or accidentally forgets his stethoscope by my bedside, only to return hours later and realise we have lots in common and should probably get married. In sickness and in health. Beautiful. I mean, Hallmark is written all over this kind of stuff. Frozen food aisles and hospital bedsides are perfect locations to meet your perfect partner, right? I know, I know. I really must stop watching movies like this.

Anyway, every moment was there. But you should know me well enough by now to know it didn't quite play out like that. It never does for girls who don't sweat glitter. Certainly, he fulfilled the role of hot single doctor very well. No ring. Not married. Come on, we all look. And I unexpectedly landed the role of mysterious single stranger. One dressed in sick-stained clothes and who seriously needed to wash. And shave. Ah yes. Hot single doctor treats hot single mess. It was as if I wasn't quite prepared for this whimsical love encounter to happen. Completely out of the blue. With no warning whatsoever.

He held my feet steady. Not in the romantic, massage-your-feet kind of way. The medical-test kind of way. And requested I looked straight into his eyes. His beautiful, big, brown eyes. In the movie, this would be the moment. The music would stop, the lighting would dim, the pace would slow and we would suddenly realise we should be together. Perfect. And, 'End scene'.

But, no. I rambled on about my bunions. *Bunions*. True story. The moment was over and with it, so was the relationship. I am the queen of awkward sometimes. No amount of editing could ever redeem that storyline. If sick-stained clothes and unruly leg hair wasn't enough, talk of bunions will surely extinguish any romantic spark. And so, after some fluids, I was sent home. One prescription. Zero phone numbers. Go figure.

After a few days, the vertigo subsided. Doctors concluded it was just an unpleasant symptom of a viral infection. But I will never forget the feeling. Everything was spinning. Everything felt like it was moving. Everything that is, but me.

As we approach the end of this journey together, allow me to be honest again with you. Sometimes I feel like I am running this race on a treadmill. Running hard. Running consistently. Running in rhythm with relationship to God. But when the day is done and I clamber back into bed again at night, everything looks the same. Everything feels the same. It's easy to feel like you are running hard, but running nowhere far. Progress is hard to see sometimes, isn't it?

We all measure progress differently. If you, like me, are a former destination girl, some days you might slip back into old habits.

Days when progress will be measured by ticking off the next thing on your list. Meeting someone special. The offer of a second date. Making it official on Facebook. But when progress is measured by our own standards, we only get deflated and defeated, disappointed and disillusioned, when circumstances remain unchanged, statuses remain single and progress seems slow. It's enough to make any girl want to hang up her running shoes.

Recently, I met a good friend for coffee. Amidst our catch up chats and laughs about my bunion chat-up lines, conversations turned to life. Our struggles. The hard stuff. I was still single. Her marriage was still difficult. On the surface, neither of us seemed much further forward than the last time we met. But as we huddled together in her car, with our takeaway McDonald's coffee cups held tightly in our weather-beaten hands, I made a comment that made us both stop to think. I said, 'I guess, sometimes if you run on the same spot for long enough, you get deeper, not further.'

I didn't intend to sound profound. But in that moment, something resonated with us and we appreciated the accidental wisdom wrapped up in this simple string of words.

Many of us define progress by our position. When we aim and we achieve. When pen can be put to paper and our next box is finally ticked. When we can sense success, because we can see success. But in the last chapter we talked about our obedience, and we learnt that obedience can sometimes seem to take us further away from our dream, not closer to it. This is true. Forward steps are not always faithful, or faith-filled, if God is not the One directing them. But a step taken in obedience is a step in the direction of God's good plan for our lives. A back-step of progress. Friend, we must learn to measure progress by a different standard. A higher standard. God's standard. Not all progress in this journey will be obvious. Not all progress in this journey will be easy. Not all progress in this journey will be instant. That's because God defines progress differently to us. Mankind often measures progress by social status. Our job status, our financial status, our relationship status. God measures progress by our heart status. Things like holiness, faithfulness, kindness, sacrifice and love. Mankind often measures progress by distance. The distance you travel up the ladder of success. God measures progress by depth. The depth of your relationship with Him. Yes, mankind often sees progress in position. Who you are as defined by human standards. Whether you are a successful businesswoman, a frequent traveller, a social media sensation, a famous author, a wife or a mother. But God sees progress in the process. Who you are destined to become in Him.

Old ways of thinking can filter into new days so easily. I constantly have to remind the journey girl in me that God infuses purpose in every single day. And tell her to grasp hold of God's gift of 'no'. To open it. To uncover it. To embrace it. But my worry is, sometimes we focus so much on God's 'no', that we neglect to see God's 'yes'. His 'no' today creates space for His 'yes' today. These two always come together. This is a package deal that can be traced back to the birth of creation recorded in the book of Genesis.

'In the beginning God created the heavens and the earth. Now the earth was formless and empty, darkness was over the surface of the deep, and the Spirit of God was hovering over the waters.'

GENESIS 1:1–2

Notice, in the beginning there was nothing. *No* thing. There were no heavens or earth, no day or night, no animals or people. Just God and a vacant space. Just God and an opportunity. For He took that which was empty and infused it with abundant purpose and activity. Because that's what He does. He sees emptiness as a blank canvas and paints a beautiful, unique picture. One full of vibrant colour and potential for growth. He sees a space waiting to be filled with something only He could imagine, only He could conceive, only He could create. He converts a place of lack into a place of life. He transforms what looks like waste into something of extraordinary worth and value. He sees potential in the void, possibility in the vacuum and purpose in the vacancy. Often it's easy to see God's 'no'. The non-existent relationship. The glaringly obvious gap in your life that used to be filled with a person you thought was 'the one'. The 'Miss' before your name and the other half that is missing. The empty seat. The quiet house. But God's 'no' for one thing is not God's 'no' to everything. God's 'no' creates space for God's 'yes'. Always. I have never noticed this before, but isn't 'no' just the first two letters of 'now'? Yes, God's 'no' is just the beginning, an opportunity, an opening, to what He wants to do right now. God's 'no' clears the stage, so He might direct the next move. His very best move for you and for me.

So let's tuck this truth in our hearts and ask one more question: What is God saying 'yes' to right now?

Remember in Chapter Two, when I finally ran to God with my breakups and He gave me the verses found in Jeremiah? Here are the verses again to remind you:

'So I went down to the potter's house, and I saw him working at the wheel. But the pot he was shaping from the clay was marred in his hands; so the potter formed it into another pot, shaping it as seemed best to him. Then the word of the LORD came to me. He said, "Can I not do with you, Israel, as this potter does?" declares the LORD. "Like clay in the hand of the potter, so are you in my hand, Israel."'

JEREMIAH 18:3–6

I take this moment to reflect on my journey so far. A journey from my broken plans to His better plans. A journey from broken dreams to beautiful destinations. But if you have reached the end of this book and you remain single, like me, you will know that better dreams do not come without their difficulties. Beautiful destinations do not come void of rough roads or tough terrain or dull days when the sun does not gloriously shine. Certainly, God's unimaginably good plan sounds good, until you realise it doesn't always feel so good getting there.

I don't like sitting on the Potter's wheel much. I'm not sure many of us do. It's confusing and complicated. Uneasy and unpredictable. Really messy and repetitively mundane. The destination girl in me wants to skip the spinning process and jump straight to the finished product. Bypass today and fast-track to my one day. Forgo the journey and arrive at the end destination. Where everything is good and everything is beautiful and everything is most definitely not spinning. Moving forwards, not moving round in circles, right?

But the journey girl in me; she sees God's fingerprint all over today and chooses to see progress from His perspective. Progress not defined by position. Progress developed in the process. Friend, a stable-born Saviour does not point to a God who is driven by destination alone. Rather, One who infuses incredible significance into every single moment that leads there too. A King seated in heavenly places does not point to a God who is finished with us as soon as we surrender our lives to Him. Rather, One who saturates each day we live on Earth with His wonderful purpose. One who sees indescribable potential in us, to shape us and develop us, so that He might use us, this side of eternity. We can't always see it. We can't always feel it. And, my goodness, we can't always make sense of it. But what if today, we chose to believe it?

Four years ago, as I mulled over the words of Jeremiah, meditated on its truth and allowed the Holy Spirit to personalise it to my heart, I picked up my pen and I wrote a poem. Like some wayward woman who turns to poetry to vent her breakups. Just call me Taylor Swift! But these words were more than just tear-filled thoughts poured onto paper. Much more. These words were drenched in truth. Truth I needed back then and truth I need right now as my hands still hold His gift of 'no'. I entitled this poem 'Something Beautiful'. Two words that had little relevance to me back then, but now, the incredible irony astounds me as I reflect on this book-writing journey. God was always crafting something beautiful. It just takes us a while to see it sometimes.

These were the words of my broken heart four years ago. These words still resound true for me today. I hope they are true for you, too.

Have there been times in your life when everything appeared
organised?

Everything headed in the direction you thought it should?

Times when everything you did seemed to go right,
and anything you put your hand to, turned out good?

I've had moments in my life like that.

And then, there are times when all of a sudden, the plans which
I have made, and have detailed down to the final part,

Are in one split moment, completely derailed and everything
I once knew seems to fall apart.

That once organised life I knew so well begins to unravel
into chaos. A disorganised mess.

And that once comforting stillness and reassuring peace,
turns into complete nothingness.

In these moments, I find myself asking God what is going on?
I even ask Him why?

Why everything I thought I knew, why my hopes and dreams
had to somehow die.

If you're like me, it's hard to feel Him. Hear Him.
God seems so distant. Far away.

Yet, it is in these very precious moments He has something
very beautiful to say.

A gentle spinning sound breaks the silence, and there I see Him.

I see a man working tirelessly. He is a Potter by trade.

Surrounded by unique and beautiful things that His very own
hands have made.

And as He gets up for just one moment, I see Him reach down
to the ground,

To lift up a piece of clay that His working hands had found.

This clay is messy. Stiff. Resistant. To man's eye it didn't look
like much,

But it slowly began to take shape under the guidance
of the Potter's touch.

I see the clay begin to soften. Take form under the movement
of His hand.

It would only be a matter of time, I thought, to see the
workings out of His master plan.

But then all of a sudden, the clay which looked promising
from the start,

Was again, collapsed on the Potter's wheel and had
completely fallen apart.

To me, this clay looked damaged. Beyond repair.
Only good to be tossed aside,

But the Potter had something beautiful intended for this clay
at the forefront of His mind.

Yes, the Potter and His plan, not destined to fail,

So He gathered the clay together again and placed it back onto

THE STRETCH OF PROGRESS

His wheel.

And the Potter kept working. As the wheel kept spinning.

Not seeming to be bothered, He had to go back
to the beginning.

And once again, the clay began to soften and it
began to take form,

As the Potter gathered together again what was now torn.

To my untrained eye, this clay was unworkable.
It appeared of no use at all.

A bit how I feel when my perfect plans fail and I seem to fall.

A mess. Useless. Battered by life's circumstances.

Directionless. Hurt. Disillusioned. Biggest failure
of the second chances.

God's plans seemingly up ahead, yet I feel stuck in reverse.

Aiming forwards. Falling backwards. And in the end,
I feel a whole lot worse.

At times, my life seems to be spinning. Trying to deal
with the struggles of each day,

And there I end up, just a hardened piece of unformed clay.

You see, a piece of clay is just that when left alone: clay.

To the untrained eye, nothing special.
Certainly nothing beautiful.

But to the eye of the Potter, all He sees is unlimited potential.

So He stretches. And He refines us. At times it's uncomfortable.
It can even hurt.

And as He starts to work with our clay, it may initially
look like it's turned out worse.

But I've come to believe this: the Potter knows exactly
what to do with His clay.

He can bring joy out of sadness. From ashes He restores beauty.

He binds up wounds. Mends brokenness. Repairs former dignity.

What seems to have been lost to the circumstances
that surround,

If given to the Potter – in Him these can be found.

So in times when things are far from perfect, when nothing
seems to be going on,

I choose to listen to the gentle spinning of the Potter's wheel
and I know that I am wrong.

For the Potter is always working; He is fashioning
something new.

And it is in those very moments when I seem to have lost
control, that this promise resounds true.

I choose to trust the Potter, as He puts His plan into action.

I choose to trust the Potter, despite doubt and fear
being my initial reaction.

I may not know what God is doing, or His intentions for me,
His clay,

But I know this: under the Potter's hand is where I want to stay.

When He looks at me, at you, His clay – do you know
what He sees?

He sees unlimited potential and endless possibilities of the
'what could be'.

So despite my circumstances. My struggles.
Despite even how I may feel,

I purposefully take my clay and I place it back onto His wheel.

Yes, it may look messy. It may hurt. Things may not be what I
had originally hoped or planned,

But I know this: something beautiful always comes
from the Potter's hand.

It's strange reading these words again a little further down the road. I remember writing each one so clearly. Wrapped up in my warm blanket on a cold winter's morning, with a scrap piece of paper and a pen in my hand. God's promise of 'something beautiful' landed on my heart, as tears landed on the page. I didn't see anything beautiful back then. You never do when surrounded by the imperfections of something incomplete and the ugliness of something unfinished.

But I am beginning to see it now. Yes, God was always working. He still is. Preparing and softening and moulding and shaping and crafting and redeeming me. You too. So that He might create something good with us. Do something good in us. Achieve something good through us. In Romans 8:29, it says:

'For those whom he foreknew he also predestined to be conformed to the image of his Son.'

In other words, for those He has singled out – that's you and that's me – His plan has always been, and will always be, to conform us, to shape us, to change us, to become more like Jesus. And each day we live is simply another opportunity to become more like Him. This is true for every believer. Single, married and everything in between. This is God's 'yes'. And God's 'yes' for us today. The longer I journey this single path, the more I realise God's good plans do not always involve a change in circumstance, but God's good plans will always involve a change in me.

Now let me say something here. I don't want you thinking that somewhere between Chapter Eight and Chapter Nine, I have suddenly welcomed the mantle of singleness and have gladly accepted that I will forever, and always, be single. This is not the case. But I have accepted I am single today. And I think that's all God asks of me for right now. Maybe that's all He asks of you today too.

But I still get it. Some days all this stretching and bending and pulling and reshaping can be a bit too much for us single girls to manage. Our faith feels pulled beyond what we think we can cope with. Our desires feel bent beyond what we think we can bear. Over the past few years, my faith has been stretched to places I never thought I would reach. I imagine your faith, too, has been stretched. So I don't want to pretend the next 24 hours will always be easy. You will know as well as I do, that some days are harder than others. Some days are uncomfortable. Unpleasant. Seriously unwanted. Sometimes it's enough to bend a girl way out of shape and feel at breaking point.

But, one day, God spoke another extraordinary message to my heart in just another ordinary moment. I was driving home from work when the reality of singleness hit me once again. I can't remember exactly what sparked this moment, but it came nonetheless. Curveballs still don't come with warning signs. But when this curveball came flying, I didn't banish my Bible to my bottom drawer or allow disappointment to drive distance between me and God. I chose a different response. A better response. A response which tells me I have changed along this journey.

I ran to God. In a moment of desperation and despair, my fragile heart cried, 'God, I don't think I can take this any more. I feel like I have reached my limit.' In the stillness, He tenderly responded, 'But isn't that the point?'

I sat in my car, perplexed by His response. Not to sound desperate or anything, but in that moment, I felt it. I so badly wanted God to change my circumstances. I wanted God to do something. Anything. And yet, this was His response. I was baffled. Confused. Until something I learnt back in school popped into my mind. Honestly, it's shocking how little I remember from school. Unless you are from Italy, I will never find your home country on a map. Never. Or unless I am using mathematics to figure out how much discount I will get on my new Italy-shaped footwear, I left most of my learning in my locker. One thing for sure is, my memory didn't trigger this thought. Which makes me point this prompt to the Holy Spirit.

As I sat in traffic, pondering and praying, I was reminded of elasticity. I know, right? Can't find the United Kingdom on a map, but this, I remember. Now, stay with me on this one. I promise, there is a point to this amateur science lesson you are about to receive. Elasticity is the ability of an object to return back to its normal shape and size after being stretched or compressed. Think of a hair bobble. And take this from a girl with much hair bobble experience. You can stretch said hair bobble to a certain point and when this stretch is released, it will return to its original state. This point is known as the elastic limit. Just throw your hair up in a messy bun and off you go. But there comes a point when this same hair bobble is stretched beyond its elastic limit. Maybe it snaps and breaks. Or goes all floppy and weird and doesn't ping back to its original shape or size. Either way, it cannot, and will not, ever go back to what it originally was. It now looks different. It possesses different qualities. It has different characteristics. It has been permanently altered. Forever changed. Never the same again.

And isn't that the point? God wants to use today to change us. Permanently change us. And so He often uses seasons we want out of, to get the best out of us. Our limitless God lovingly uses difficult days to stretch us. Maybe even stretch us to our limit. Our elastic limit. So He might change us. Better us. Improve us. Make us more like Jesus. He wants us to have different qualities and different characteristics. He wants us to leave today different than how we entered, and face tomorrow different than how we faced today. God values our character over our comfort. He sees beneath any surface level progress and He digs deep to uncover beauty in those unseen areas of our lives. He stretches us and bends us and pulls us and reshapes us, so He might remake us into something good. Something beautiful.

And although you may feel like you have reached your limit today, you will never reach His. How many times have you heard the words of Philippians 4:13? 'I can do all things through him who strengthens me' (ESV). But there is something so sweet about this verse I want to share with you. In Greek, this verse is better translated as 'I have strength for all things'. Not to *do* all things. But *for* all things. How such a small word can make such a big difference.

You see, some days His strength will certainly help you do things. Achieve things. Big things. Some days, you will stand up against giants, face your adversities, walk through fire, climb up mountains and victoriously dance straight into your dreams. God can, and God will, give you strength to do such things. You are not only *designed* to thrive where God has you today, you are *equipped* to thrive there too. But sometimes, His strength is not so that you might do something mighty, but that you might bear something difficult. Friend, even though I come to the end of this book and I have changed in many ways, some days I still cry because I am single. Yes, it's still hard. But let's allow the words of Paul in Philippians to rest in our hearts. Apply this promise to our lives as we wrestle with our single girl struggles and continue on this journey towards God's beautiful plans for our lives. Here's what I've learnt. Sometimes His strength will help you wait in a season of want, when all you want to do is run ahead or run away. Sometimes His strength will allow you to stand in the middle of an obstacle, not instantly overcome it. Sometimes His strength will sustain you in the valley, not help you climb out of it. Yes. Enough strength to survive. Enough stability to stand. Enough energy to endure. Today, you too, might feel a stretch of faith. Allow me to reach from behind my secondhand laptop, hold your hand and whisper an honest and vulnerable, 'Me too'. I feel stretched too. But God will use a stretch of faith to stretch us. A stretch that will change us. A stretch that will permanently change us. This is the stretch of progress.

The apostle Paul knew what it was like to be on the mountaintop and in the valley. To be in plenty and in want. To be well fed and to be hungry. To be on the platform and to be in prison. He also knew what it was like to be single. Friend, you have God's strength for all things today. Hold on to this promise, as God holds onto you. You are strong enough to get through this 24-hour period. You will be stronger still for what comes next. Yes. He has prepared you for today. He is preparing you for tomorrow.

Think of young David. He spent day after day in a field looking after sheep. I imagine, every day felt the same. I imagine, every day looked the same. Feeding sheep. Guiding sheep. Shaving sheep. Protecting sheep. Serenading sheep. And whatever other sheep duties shepherd people got up to in those days. And when the sun began to fade, he journeyed back home to his family. He drifted off to sleep, only to repeat the same routine all over again. Day after day.

Until, one day, a man named Samuel interrupted David's norm and everything changed. Extraordinary moments are often birthed in the middle of the ordinary and mundane. And although we are never specifically told what David thought when Samuel anointed him as next King of Israel in 1 Samuel 16, my guess is, this young shepherd boy didn't feel prepared for such a high calling.

But God doesn't see progress in position. He sees progress in the process. Little did David know that every day he practised playing his harp, that one day he would skilfully play his harp for King Saul. This was the promise of God in motion. Little did David know that every day he went to work to look after a flock of sheep, that one day he would look after a nation and lead an entire army. This was the promise of God in motion. Little did David know that every day he picked up his shepherd boy sling to master his aim and train his eye, he would one day aim this same sling towards an enemy and watch him fall in defeat. This was the promise of God in motion. Little did David know that every day he fought a bear or a lion to protect his sheep, that one day he would be strong enough to fight many battles and conquer many opponents. This was the promise of God in motion. David was prepared for each day, and David was being prepared for tomorrow. Because that's what God does.

Think of young Joseph. A man with a dream. A God-given dream. But brotherly hatred found Joseph in a pit and later sold as a servant to work in Potiphar's house. Things went from bad to worse and the lies of Potiphar's wife soon left Joseph lying in prison. Distant dreams can often look like disasters. And yet, in both situations we read, 'the LORD gave Joseph success in everything he did' (Gen. 39:3,23).

Yes, Joseph found favour with God *and* also found himself

179

working as a slave. Joseph found success in God *and* also found himself stuck in a cell. Deep pits and lying wives and prison walls don't exactly scream progress, do they? Until we remember God sees progress differently to us.

You see, God used the deep pit to direct Joseph towards the dream. This was the promise of God in motion. God used the lies of Potiphar's wife to align Joseph with His perfect plan. This was the promise of God in motion. God used the prison walls to prepare Joseph for palace work and position him for tomorrow's promise. This was the promise of God in motion. The boy who flaunted his dream to his family needed a little reshaping. Time to grow in maturity and develop in humility. This was the promise of God in motion. Joseph was prepared for each day, and Joseph was being prepared for tomorrow. Because that's what God does.

Friend, if you have ever wondered what God is doing right now, you are not alone. Sometimes today just doesn't make sense. Not one bit. But we have this assurance: God knows. He knows what we need today and He knows what we need tomorrow too. He has 'prevision' for our provision. Truth is, many of us are striving for something we cannot yet survive. When I look back over the past few years, I admit, being single has been the best thing for me. I had many unhealthy attitudes and unhelpful perspectives that would have remained completely untouched if God had answered my prayers the way I wanted. Might the same be true for you today?

People say the best kind of exercise is the kind of exercise you will do. We all know running is not my thing, but a few years ago I signed up to the gym and I kind of liked it. I know. I judge me too. Honestly, I used to look at people who enjoyed exercise and wonder what was wrong with them, but exercise-induced endorphins is the real deal. Who knew, right?

But if you have ever been to the gym before, or exerted yourself in some physical way, you will know how important it is to complete a warm-up first. If you don't, you might cause injury or pull a muscle or really struggle to get off the toilet seat for a few days. Not that I have firsthand experience of this or anything. But if you stretch, you can often lift heavier, bend further, squat lower, accelerate faster and reach higher.

So, what if we applied this same principle to right now? What if today is our warm-up? What if today is our stretch? Sometimes this journey will leave you feeling overwhelmed by life and underwhelmed by progress. Some days, all we will want to do is stop. Give up. Give in. Hang up our running shoes and bow out of the race. Jeremiah knew this feeling too. In Jeremiah 12, he comes to God with many questions. Questions I, too, have asked many times. 'God, what are you planning here?' 'God, why are not doing anything?' 'God, how long must this go on for?' God's response to Jeremiah is somewhat unexpected. And yet today, there is unexpected strength found within His words for you and me. God replied, 'If you have raced with men on foot, and they have wearied you, how will you compete with horses?' (Jer. 12:5).

Oh, sweet friend, allow this verse to settle your heart today. You were not designed to only race with men on foot. You were destined to run with horses. God has bigger things, better things, more beautiful things, ahead of you. More than that which you could ever imagine for yourself. But what if the only way to get to better things tomorrow, is to accept bigger challenges today? What if you race with men on foot today, so that one day you can run with horses? Today's stretch is tomorrow's strength. This is the stretch of progress.

Right now, I invite you to take a moment. To look back over your journey so far and consider the things you have learnt. The attitudes that have changed. The steps you have taken. Maybe you are a lot less worried about tomorrow and a lot more present today. This is a stretch of progress. Maybe someone in your world recently got engaged, or married. Instead of allowing comparison to drive you to compete, or criticise, or copy, you chose a different response. To celebrate her. To complement her. To cheer for her. This is another stretch of progress. Maybe instead of reaching for your phone this morning, you reached for God's Word. This is a stretch of progress. Or maybe you stepped forwards in faith, or stepped back in obedience, because God simply asked you to. This is another stretch of progress. Good progress. And progress looks so beautiful on you.

Today, I celebrate with you. But I also want to challenge you. Keep your running shoes on. Tighten up those laces. Take each stride in faith, no matter how small it might seem. Because one day, God will invite you to run with horses, and you will be so glad you did.

CHAPTER 10

To Me. From Me.

Yes.

We made it.

I can hardly believe it. To begin a book was never something I thought to achieve. To finish a book was never something I thought I could achieve. Yet, here we are. Sharing final thoughts together. What a journey. For me, this journey has been filled with glorious highs and extreme lows. A lot of learning invades every page and a whole lot of living saturates every sentence. But one thing for sure is, this story, my story, will continue long after I type the final word in this chapter. And, sweet friend, your story will continue too.

At the start of this book, I invited you to come on this journey with me. But I was clear. This message was for me, as much as it was intended for you. And do you know something? I was so right. I never knew how much I desperately needed to write these words. But God did. He always does.

Right now, my relationship status remains unchanged. But, in many ways, I am changed. In many other ways, I am still changing. I wish I could press rewind and speak to my younger self. I would pull up a chair and invite her to sit with me. Hold her hand. Give her tissues when needed. Tell her everything I know now. If this was possible, I think this is what I would say:

To the girl who followed the gentle nudge of God to purchase a secondhand laptop. The girl with absolutely no idea how to write a book. I would tell her: she doesn't need to know the details when she trusts the One who does.

To the girl with broken bones and broken dreams. I would tell her: God cares. God so deeply cares about her breakups. Run to Him, not from Him. Broken things are the beginning of beautiful things when placed into the right hands.

To the girl sitting on the tram with no clue where she is going. I would tell her to trust God. For He has never failed her yet. Broken plans are just God's better plans under construction. Oh, and I would also tell her it's weird to keep teeth in a memories box.

To the girl waiting for her tomorrows. I would tell her: God is working today. Don't allow tomorrow's dream to become today's distraction. Recognise. Remind. Redirect. Recalibrate. Repeat. And always check the sat-nav is in the car before driving anywhere.

Otherwise you will get lost.

To the girl with the messy bun and the freckled face. I would tell her: God thinks she is beautiful. Unpretty is not a word, and certainly not a word He would ever use to describe her.

To the girl on the plane trying to run away from home. I would tell her: God is waiting on the other side. He always will be. His heart beats for her and longs for her to stay close. Every single day.

To the girl surrounded by other people's good news. I would remind her to flip the script. To complete, not compete. To celebrate, not criticise. To complement, not copy. There will be a day when she will say 'congratulations' and it won't be fake. It won't feel forced. It will be genuine words from a genuine heart that understands she is singled out by her loving God.

To the girl debilitated by decisions. I would tell her: God's good plan is not dependent on her getting it right every single time. Instead, He invites her on a journey with Him. An adventure. Just Father and daughter together.

To the girl holding the unwanted gift of 'no'. I would tell her: this gift is good, because the Giver is good. Don't allow half truths to strip the goodness of this full truth. Uncover this gift. Unwrap this gift. Unpack this gift. Use this gift. God's 'no' is just the beginning of what He is doing right now.

And to the girl wondering what God is doing today. I would tell her to trust the process. Progress is not determined by position; progress is developed in the process. Stay on His wheel. He is crafting something good. Something beautiful. Oh, and it is never OK to use the word 'bunion' in a chat-up line. Ever.

As I sit here to write these final words, there is just one more person I feel compelled to write to. The girl I will be tomorrow.

I don't think about her half as much as I used to, but some days my thoughts still wander and my mind still wonders what she will be like. Will she ever meet someone? Will she ever marry? Will she ever be a mother? I still don't know the answer to these questions. But I do know this: God's plans for her are always better and His promise is something beautiful.

Love God, Love All

Waverley Abbey Trust is a ministry, equipping you to love God, love your neighbour and love yourself.

Through our portfolio of courses and plethora of resources, you can learn to be the difference in society.

Our free Bible reading notes help you to draw closer to Jesus and by living every day with Jesus, we believe you can foster the foundation to help and serve others.

waverleyabbeytrust.org

Learn to be the Difference

You'll find space to learn and grow alongside a strong Christian heritage. Waverley Abbey College provides training that ranges from one day seminars up to five-year part-time Higher Education courses in:

- Counselling
- Spiritual Formation
- Contemporary Chaplaincy
- Theology
- Leadership

"It was a brilliant experience; the peaceful and positive atmosphere at Waverley; the friendships formed; the supportive tutors; the course material; the practical work and the encouragement."

- David Cunliffe, graduate

To find out more about any of our courses, check out our website. Or come and visit us for an open day. Register your interest here

waverleyabbeycollege.ac.uk

Fresh ways to engage your small groups

Are you looking for new ideas for your small groups? Why not shake up the cycle with something different?

Andy Peck has three insightful seminars to get your small groups thinking. Try:

Renewing your Mind
Discover how the Bible's view of the mind overlaps with neuroscience

Understanding the Bible in today's world
Learn tools for wise interpretation and application

Building community through small groups
Develop biblical community with godly leadership

Andy's visiting churches all over the UK with these seminars.
If you'd like him to come to you, please get in touch at
waverleyabbeyresources.org/contact-us